I Thought Mommy
Didn't Want Me Anymore:

A Story of Broken Attachment and Spiritual Recovery

Robert F. R. Peters, Jr.

Bilbo Books Publishing
www.BilboBooks.com
bilbobookspublishing@gmail.com

ISBN- 978-1-7326180-3-9
1-7326180-3-8

Printed in the United States of America

All rights reserved. Published in the United States of America by Bilbo Books Publishing. Athens, Georgia

Topics: personal memoir, religion, mental health

Dedication

To my Mom,
Whose love, fortitude
and gentle spirit
were beyond measure

and my Dad,
Who carried with grace,
unexpected challenges in
a life of service

Table of Contents

Preface

THIS BOOK IS A STORY OF REBIRTH AND RENEWAL. It begins in my childhood at age six and a half when my mother was stricken with a possible life-threatening illness just before she delivered my third sibling. She was hospitalized for nearly two months. The effects of her absence affected both of us because my childhood attachment with her was significantly altered. The change in our relationship produced the feeling expressed in the title of this memoir. Early in my life that feeling was repressed until I discovered it in the episode recounted in the first chapter.

As a young teenager in the 1950s, I was fearful of psychology, psychiatrists and mental health issues. I saw frightening stories in Life magazine in my home about people incarcerated in psychiatric institutions, dealing with severe mental illness. At times, I worried about whether someone might suggest I was in need of such treatment, wondering if, somehow, I had some unknown mental flaw. I kept such fears to myself, vowing I would avoid psychiatry. The stigma connected with mental health issues in the 1950s was very much alive in my youthful mind. In my first year of college, I took a course in psychology and decided that it was about understanding how the mind and emotions work, and that I need not be fearful.

One of the important learnings from my experience is that the methods of psychotherapy have advanced dramatically since 1944 when my last sibling was born. Asking for help from a skilled therapist is a healthy decision. It is a sign of wisdom to acknowledge the need for professional help to address emotional and mental health issues, just as it is wise to seek medical help for physical illnesses. In my mid-seventies, I sought the help of a therapist to address what I thought was difficulty with a lack of motivation to do things I thought I wanted to do. I discovered the long-held pain of my childhood trauma.

This memoir about my life and recovery from trauma grew from two motives. The first was a personal desire to record for myself the events and the impact of my work in therapy. At various times throughout my life, I have maintained a journal. It was an invaluable aid in recalling this story. When I started to write, I had no intention of sharing the story with anyone. This was to be no more than my personal record.

But the situation changed. My therapist began to suggest that sharing my experience in facing and dealing with addiction and depression could be of value to others. Moreover, she felt the story and the process might also be of value to mental health professionals in relation to the long-term effects which can result from interrupted or altered childhood attachment. This narrative describes how I idealized my view of my family. It is also the story of how the trauma led me to engage in self-defeating behaviors which led to depression, addiction and more. To regain my mental and emotional health, it was necessary to transform an idealized vision of my family's story into a realistic and healthier understanding of its truth and impact on all of us, and to take responsibility for the pain and hurt I caused. My therapist has said it is a story about "all the messiness of the human condition." It also is about a variety of everyday events and pleasures. An occasional poem appears as well.

One of the beauties of creation is that each of us must find our own pathway to fulfillment. How each person understands and relates to the world is determined, in significant ways, by how we experienced and responded to our first attachment to our primary caregivers, usually, but not always, our mothers. The story of the journey in this book is a significant part of my discovering and coming to terms with the ways in which a traumatic childhood experience affected the relationship with Mom, my ensuing emotional development, my career, and the lives of each person in my family. It is my hope that there will be readers who find elements of the story which resonate with their own experiences. If, in the end, you find yourself curious about your own earliest attachment and its influence on your life, that will be an extra bonus.

Frederick, Maryland
May, 2019

Acknowledgements

THREE SKILLED, SENSITIVE THERAPISTS HELPED ME FIND AND UNPACK THE SOURCES AND CONSEQUENCES OF THE TRAUMA IN MY CHILDHOOD. They include Dr. A., clinical psychologist and my primary therapist; L.R., a Licensed Clinical Social worker who guided me through treatment for post-traumatic stress using a therapy process known by its initials, EMDR; and P.T., also a Licensed Clinical Social Worker who, in 1991, first found the edges of my childhood stress but could not continue the work, in part because I did not resume our sessions. Of course, neither Mom or Dad meant to inflict emotional trauma. It just happened because of Mom's illness.

I owe a sincere and large thank-you to three clergy friends, Doug Griffin, Carolyn Roberts, and Fred Wenner. Each of them reviewed the draft and made suggestions for changes which helped make "the rough places plain." I am indebted to them. A special word goes to my editors, Bill Bray and Bowen Craig, of Bilbo Books Publishing whose experience and detailed editing helped weed out myriad typographical errors and offered helpful word changes. Heather Bodner, a gifted graphics designer, produced the compelling cover to the book. Paul Mitchell, editor of the St. Lawrence Plaindealer, the weekly newspaper in Canton, New York, gave permission to reprint my article, March in a Sleeping Sugarbush, first published in March, 1972. The Rev. Dr. James Crawford, former Senor Minister at Old South Church in Boston gave permission to reprint portions of his sermon, "In the Eye of the Hurricane." I am grateful to Cowley Publications for granting permission to use quotations from Centering Prayer and Inner Awakening, by Cynthia Bourgeault. My thanks to Steven Lehner for the back cover photo.

I owe a special thank-you to my wife, Ginny, who did the initial proof reading and saved me from many embarrassing typographical errors. Beyond her attention to detail, I am deeply grateful for her patience as I have traveled this journey. Her encouragement and support have underscored the importance of the work. In the long run, our marriage has been made richer and more vibrant because I found new vitality and joy in living the years which remain for us. This journey, traveled together, has enlarged my understanding and perceptions of what love can be when it is cultivated and nourished and aided, when needed, by the support and care of skilled therapists. Many people have contributed to my recovery and revitalized spiritual journey. I am grateful to them all.

Chapter 1

Meeting the Unexpected

L<small>ITTLE DID</small> I <small>KNOW WHAT WAS TO COME IN</small> A<small>UGUST</small> 2009 <small>WHEN</small> I <small>ARRANGED AN APPOINTMENT WITH A CLINICAL PSYCHOLOGIST.</small> This was to be the first of what I expected would be three or four sessions to address a nagging lack of self-motivation. For weeks, I had felt little energy to pursue the projects I had set for myself. In April and May, I completed the last of my consulting contracts.

In June, my wife and I drove from Virginia to Ohio to visit one of my two best friends from high school days, followed by a week at the biennial national meeting of the United Church of Christ in Grand Rapids, Michigan. This was an intense time. I had a role in helping to draft a major resolution submitted to the delegates. In Atlanta in 2005, I voted for a resolution supporting marriage equality for LGBTQ people. That was an emotional vote cast in memory of my late brother, Gregory, who was gay. In 2007, I was part of the meeting which celebrated the 50th anniversary of our church. In 1957, my father was a delegate to the founding meeting of the new United Church of Christ. It was inspiring to be part of celebrating the first half century of the new church.

After this event, I was free to turn my attention to the things I wanted to do, and yet, they remained untouched as the days and weeks went by. An atmosphere of malaise and un-interestedness had come over me. I felt no motivation to do much of anything.

The appointment with Dr. A. was set for Friday morning, August 14. As I drove to her office, a sense of apprehension began to grow. The closer I came, the more agitated the butterflies in my stomach became. Arriving in the parking lot several minutes early, I stayed in the car until moments before the scheduled appointment.

Once in the waiting room, I thumbed through a *National Geographic* magazine, not really reading the articles. The photographs provided a distraction and the butterflies began to quiet down. After a few minutes, Dr. A. opened the door to the inner suite of offices and greeted me with a warm "Hi Rob." She led me along a short hallway to her first-floor office. It was appointed in a plain way, softly lit with a couple of lamps.

The room conveyed a sense of calm. Immediately to my right was a white sofa with its back to the wall and facing to my left. A small, burgundy colored throw pillow rested at each end. A square side table was just beyond the end of the sofa. It held an open box of tissues. The long wall across the from the door we had entered consisted of large, tinted windows. They faced a parking lot and beyond it a sizable cluster of trees, their leaves stirred by a soft summer breeze. On this sunny day, they added to the serenity of the room.

A small desk was along the wall to the left of the doorway we had entered. It faced toward the open end of the room. Dr. A. offered me a seat on the sofa. She sat on an armless black, straight-back office chair facing me. A comfortable, upholstered armchair was to her left. Its position created a triangle, as if an unknown guest was expected.

When I first asked for an appointment, I explained my lack of interest in doing the things I thought I wanted to do. Now, as we began our conversation, she invited me to say more about this lack of motivation. I began to describe it, but had difficulty finding words. She started to ask me a question.

"*Please,*" I said. "*Don't talk for a moment. I feel very tense. Something strange is happening. I don't know what, but a strange sadness is growing.*"

"Tell me where you feel it. Where in your body?"

"*It started in my stomach, but it's going to my chest. It's not physical pain, it's a sadness in my heart. I feel like I don't want to do this.*"

"Don't push it down. Let it come. Stay with it."

"*But I don't want to. It's too painful.*"

And still the tightness in my throat kept coming. My eyes were filling with tears, welling up. The sadness was overpowering. I couldn't stop it. Now, racked with weeping and uncontrolled emotional pain, I reached for the small throw pillow next to me, wrapping my arms around it and hugging it to myself, as if trying to protect myself from some terrible, unknown thing. This was a frightening, awful and all-encompassing sadness like none I had ever felt.

I heard Dr. A. say: "Take deep breaths." With several gulping inhalations, the worst of the waves of sadness started to ease. My arms stayed crossed over the throw pillow, and I kept hugging it tightly, still frightened by this tidal wave of sadness. Slowly, with each deep breath, the sadness began to ebb. We sat in silence until composure returned.

Tear-flooded eyes looked at Dr. A. *"Where did all this sadness come from? Will I ever feel happy again?"* Her kind and gentle face looked back at me. "It's the answer to those questions we will explore together."

I began to sense and describe a deep regret that my Dad had missed the past nineteen years of my life. He died of lung cancer on March 6, 1990 at age eighty-one, three months short of his eighty-second birthday. I was fifty-three. He died not knowing about the things I had accomplished after his death: earning a Doctor of Ministry degree at Lancaster Theological Seminary in 1998, serving as Executive Director of the Boston Seamen's Friend Society from January 1997 to May of 2000, being chosen as a part-time Parish Associate, a pastoral care position at Rock Spring United Church of Christ in Arlington, Virginia from October 2003 to January 2005. These were some of the elements of a long journey back to a restored career in new forms of ministry. Sadly, Dad did not know of them.

Over the years we had developed a relationship that was warm and mutual, especially after he retired and moved to a not-for-profit retirement community. He was an active volunteer there, editing the community's monthly newsletter. My own experience with not-for-profit organizations gave us some common ground. This was especially true when I lived in Chattanooga, only ninety miles from Mom and Dad's home in Pleasant Hill. Now, once again, the feelings of loss were stark. I really missed him.

There were other stories of loss as well: my mother's death in 2000 at age ninety-two; my brother Greg's death from cirrhosis of the liver at age fifty-seven in 2001. The litany of losses included lost jobs and the break-up of what I thought was my engagement to a college sweetheart. She had found someone else while I was gone to the Philippines for a junior year of study abroad. To these were added the years of alcohol addiction before I found sobriety and the regrets I carried about its effects on people I loved. (More of that story later.)

As this first therapy session came to an end, I realized that, for years, I was carrying a deep, unnamed sadness which blocked me from feeling joy and fulfillment. Dr. A. assured me that one day I would be able to affirm this sadness and understand its source and meaning. But how could I "affirm" sadness? How could I live through it in order to come to a new place? The possibility seemed beyond anything imaginable. The past, with its broken dreams and losses, along with some affirming accomplishments, was done. This deep sadness, unrecognized until this painful hour, had blocked me from finding new avenues of activity and living which might bring new purpose in life. Now, leaving the therapist's office, I could only wonder what could overcome this stunning sadness.

A day or two after this therapy session, a daydream captured my imagination. It consisted of fantasies of wanting to feel as alive, exuberant and as involved as I had felt in my first two years at Yale Divinity School. In those days, all the dreams of a wonderful career in ministry were alive. Study was fulfilling, and the work of preparing to become an ordained pastor in a local congregation fully occupied my attention and energy.

Four days after the first appointment, the second occurred. The focus turned to my up-and-down employment history. During those years, and now again as I looked back, much of it seemed to be little more than an ongoing struggle to survive and provide for a family. The previous session's connection to sadness appeared again when recalling once more that Dad had not seen my career moves since 1990, including three and a half years in Boston before retiring in May of 2000.

The discussion with Dr. A. turned to the many volunteer activities which were consuming so much time. They were keeping me from doing the

4

things I said I want to do: be it in my woodshop or work on family genealogy. The list of volunteer activities seemed endless: weekly rehearsal with the choir at Little River United Church of Christ and involvement with the Stewardship committee, attending monthly meetings of the United States Coast Guard Auxiliary flotilla to which my wife, Ginny, and I belonged, serving as chair of the church development committee with the Central Atlantic Conference of the United Church of Christ, member of the Board of Directors for the Potomac Association of the UCC, active member of the UCC-related Pillar of Faith Awards committee at Howard University School of Divinity and participating with Ginny in activities of the Mount Vernon Democratic Committee. In addition, I had been asked again to direct a feasibility study and church capital campaign as a consultant. All of these, together with everyday responsibilities for the care of house and yard, were blocking me from doing what I claimed I really wanted to do.

Dr. A. asked me to take part in a role play. First, she had me sit in the vacant upholstered chair to my right, and to act as if I were an outsider speaking to me. I was to tell Rob that he should give up various of the volunteer activities (specifically naming several of them) so that he can get to other things he wants to do: writing family stories for grandkids, doing genealogical research and finishing boat models he started years ago.

Then, directed back to my usual seat on the sofa, she asked: "How does it make you feel to hear the suggestion that you should give up your volunteer jobs so you can do the things you say you want to do?"

Very strange feelings arose. *"Giving them up makes me feel I might become invisible. What would I matter anymore? Giving them up makes me feel: So what good am I? I want to be recognized. Letting go of my volunteer things means I will become invisible."*

As the session ended, the therapist pointed out that I was placing a load on myself trying to sort through my feelings and my sense of being "down" or 'blocked," and at the same time trying to sort through a lot of stuff about family history. (I also had been wanting to sort and preserve two sets of letters which both sets of my grandparents had written from their homes in Ohio to Mom and Dad during the 1930s and early 1940s when my family lived in Bridgeport, Connecticut.) I began to see that I wanted to do far more than time would allow, and these hidden fears of being "invisible" and "not mattering" were leaving me both conflicted and unable to decide how to proceed.

A month later, in mid-September, the pressure came to a head. As I was driving from Mt. Vernon to my therapy session, the sadness started to churn again somewhere near the middle of my stomach. Dr. A.'s first question was to ask how I had been in the weeks since our last session. The intervening days had seen the death and funeral of Senator Ted Kennedy. The coverage had included the story of his effort to recover from addiction and redeem the dark aspects of his young adulthood, to remake his life. He affirmed that part of his redemption came with the help of his second wife, whom he called "the love of my life."

I realized how important my wife is to my continuing recovery. Now, in response to Dr. A.'s question, my current feelings and the still-present sadness-of-heart rose up. My reply was that I was regretting my broken career in ministry, the breakup of my first marriage and family (of my own doing, years before I faced my addiction), and the pain I caused all those I loved. The words tumbled out: *"How will I ever be able to find redemption or forgiveness?"*

As we talked, I sensed that, as I started to say "no" to some of the activities that have so filled my time, the realization was dawning that having so many activities was providing a way to keep from having to meet myself. The many feelings of sadness have been hidden under a relentless effort to rebuild some kind of respectable career so that what I am on the inside will match what I try to appear to be to others on the outside. Backing away from many of these activities means I will have to meet myself all over again.

Several hours after this session, when thinking about sad times in my life, a particularly startling occurrence came to mind. It happened on a Sunday morning in the spring of 1985 during a visit with my parents in Pleasant Hill, Tennessee. While showering and preparing to attend church,

6

I suddenly was overwhelmed with an overpowering grief about the death of my grandfather Peters. This sudden pain flared up in spite of the fact he had been dead more than twenty-four years. (I knew his death happened in the winter during my second year in seminary, and learned later it was on Sunday, February 19, 1961.)

Now, in 1985, I was weeping over the fact that he had died without seeing me graduate from seminary. I had never had a chance to talk with him about my theological studies, or how my training differed from his, or about how he had experienced his first years in ministry. Even though I had made the trip to Ohio to attend his funeral, the pain of his loss stayed hidden until some unanticipated trigger let loose a torrent of unrelieved grieving. It was so vivid I could not keep it to myself. After showering that Sunday morning, I let Mom and Dad know what had happened. We had no conversation about my feelings or what they meant. We simply went to church.

A major step in the process of "meeting myself all over again" happened four weeks later in a session on October 23, 2009. It was a momentous and life-changing discovery. For this session, I took with me a newspaper photo which had touched me when I saw it earlier in September. It was a first-day-of-school photo. In it, a young mother was standing with her two sons outside an elementary school, putting her arms around the boys as they nestled against her. The boys were about seven and eight years old. The mother's head was tilted forward and down, her eyes gazing at them. The picture conveyed the emotion of a loving mother gathering her offspring into a safe place before sending them off to school. As she gazed at them, her face revealed to me a deep sense of caring, warmth and safety. The face of each boy conveyed deep feelings of security, safety and love.

When I first saw the picture, it touched me so deeply, I began to cry. I felt immediately a yearning for, a wishing for, having had similar feelings with my own Mom. Now, being shown the photo, my therapist asked me: "What do you feel when you look at the picture?" The first word was "Warmth." I talked more about it and what I had not felt with Mom: not being able to recall similar feelings. I noted that it had always seemed as if my schoolwork was never quite good enough. If I brought home papers with mistakes on them, she sometimes would say "but you knew the answer to that." I sensed in such moments I was being judged, rather than encouraged.

My thoughts turned to the experience of my Mom's illness when my youngest brother, Greg, was born in February, 1944. I was 6 years old, three months short of age seven. Alan had been born in May of 1942, and Frank in April of 1940. We were living in Bridgeport, Connecticut and had moved to a larger house the previous October because of the growing family. The crisis began on January 24 when Mom was taken to the hospital, suffering from a creeping tingling and paralysis impacting her legs. Gradually, it progressed until her lower body was paralyzed. At the time it was thought to be a form of poliomyelitis. Actually, her illness most likely was what is known today as Guillian-Barre syndrome, a creeping paralysis which begins in the lower legs and slowly ascends the body. It can be life-threatening, and often leaves side effects. It did with Mom. For a while, the concern was that the paralysis would reach her diaphragm, affect her breathing and necessitate the use of an iron lung to force breathing. This surely would have killed the baby.

Mom's physician, whose name I have never forgotten, Dr. Stella Strayer, saw Mom through the delivery by natural childbirth without the use of any sedation because of the uncertainty of its potential dire effects. Fearing the presence of poliomyelitis, infant Gregory was taken immediately from Mom to the hospital nursery and kept away from her for some period due to the polio fear. I don't know the detail of when Greg was able to be placed in Mom's arms, but I do know he was denied much of the earliest bonding that needs to take place between an infant and its mother.

After seven weeks in the hospital, Mom came home, still suffering from continuing pain and tingling in her face. For a long time, she was not able to have anyone be near her face or touch it. For weeks she was not able to hold new-born Gregory for fear he would touch her pained face. Quoting from my journal entry for the October 23rd therapy session:

As I talked about her illness and not feeling warmth from Mom, I began to feel very uncomfortable. I wanted to not talk about it and said so. Dr. A. said: stay with the feeling. It's a natural avoidance to not want to talk about it.

Stay with it. You are a little boy six or seven. What are you feeling?'

A long pause ensued. Then the words came: **"It feels like Mommy doesn't want me anymore."** The tears began to come. I blurted: **"Why doesn't she want me?"** And then the pain and the tears were uncontrollable. I reached for the throw pillow next to me and wrapped my arms around it tightly. With the tears and the pain streaming down, I was reliving a pain, a hurt and a sadness that had been buried for seven decades. In the midst of the pain, I managed to murmur: *"but it wasn't her fault. It wasn't her fault she got sick."* Once again, the tears and grieving were intense. Several minutes passed while the intensity of the emotions lessened and some composure returned.

Gradually, I was able to explain some of the circumstances affecting our family during this crisis. For the seven weeks Mom was in the hospital, Dad had to try to balance his work as a minister with caring for three young boys. At some point Grandmother Caris came on the train from Columbus, Ohio to help care for us, and Mom's Aunt Rachel came from Trenton, New Jersey for part of the time. I don't remember anything about their presence. After Mom came home, an article about her illness, extraordinary natural childbirth and the near miraculous recovery appeared in the *Bridgeport Sunday Herald* for March 5, 1944. It is reprinted on the next page.

I was astounded at what had happened in this latest intense and very painful session. It was very difficult to absorb what I had discovered, but it was clearly true. This childhood pain, brought on by believing I was not wanted after my mother's illness, had been buried for a very long time. Dr. A. explained that what I experienced was childhood trauma, and it resulted in many of the same effects which are now observed in those who suffer post-traumatic stress (PTS). As I was beginning to learn, this traumatic experience changed the way I related to my mother and other people, and, as I was to discover, over the course of the next seven decades produced a

Baby's Born As Paralysis is Conquered
By ETHEL BECKWITH

Some babies will take the hard way to getting born but this is a story of one who found he couldn't trick anybody at Bridgeport Hospital.

He is the fourth son of the Rev. and Mrs. Peters of Park Street Congregational Church.

Although he was born Feb. 2, The Herald is the first to announce that his 100% arrival marked an amazing feat in local medical history.

HIT BY PARALYSIS

The minister's wife was afflicted 10 days before the birth with a form of paralysis.

It is not infantile paralysis but a virus that affects the nerve centers.

Mrs. Peters, when brought to the hospital, could scarcely move and was in acute pain because of this affiliation.

Since anesthetic slows respiration, her doctor, Dr. Estella M. Strayer, faced a dilemma.

She called on Dr. William German, noted neurologist of New Haven, and Dr. Crawford Griswold, Bridgeport obstetrician.

Dr. German was leaving to join the navy. He was prevailed upon to come to the local hospital for consultation with Drs. Strayer and Griswold.

Helpless and inert while her pain increased, the invalid didn't know that the decision was to make the delivery without any anesthetic, on the big chance that the baby at least would survive.

Dr. Strayer, resolved to save both, had an iron lung ready for Mrs. Peters.

Beside it was an oxygen tent, while the Rev. Mr. Peters and two friends stood ready to offer transfusions. The Dr. kept telling Mrs. Peters as she demanded anesthetic, "Any minute now – any minute," while the boy took his time – he was six hours arriving.

Precarious moments passed when it was not known whether either of the two lives involved could take it.

WEIGHS NINE POUNDS

Dr. Strayer was no less jubilant than the minister when the boy, who henceforth shall be Gregory Peters, presented his appearance, weighing nine pounds.

Rallying better than expected, Mrs. Peters did not require the iron lung but was placed in an oxygen tent where she received the three transfusions.

Still it was three or four days before it could be certain that the strain on the paralyzed body was within human endurance.

The story goes now into its happy-ending phase. Mrs. Peters is learning to walk, using a "walker" such as supports the weak legs of children.

Slowly, she is recovering from the pre-birth illness, known as periradiculitis, or inflammation of the nerve-roots.

The children are being cared for by the mother of Mrs. Peters, who was formerly Mary Caris.

Naturally the pleased pastor is stirred to a sermon. "It proved to me," he says, "the essential goodness of people. But I can tell you it was terrifying."

As a friend of the family, Dr. Strayer presents him with both his wife and baby as a present.

"We could never repay her," says the pastor.

This is a transcription of the article which appeared in the Bridgeport Sunday Herald, on March 5, 1944. A photograph of the original appears at the end of the chapter. My Dad's marginal note of the date is visible in the margin.

profound effect on how I viewed myself.

It was becoming clear that therapy would not be a short-term process to regain a lack of motivation to do the projects I had on my list. I realized we were embarked on a lengthy journey to discover the effects of Mom's illness not only on my life, but also its effects on the entire family. I was learning that I had lived for many years with varying degrees of depression.

Before this session ended, Dr. A. asked me if I had practiced meditation in the course of my life. I had not. She assured me that in coming sessions, she would share with me some meditation techniques that might help to lift the "down" times I experienced from time to time.

I drove home emotionally exhausted. I knew from having studied the counseling techniques of Dr. Carl Rogers in a seminary course on pastoral counseling that I had been through what could be called "a critical episode in psychotherapy." It did not frighten me, rather it amazed me that I had experienced such a profound event, and yet, its effects had remained unknown to me for more than seven decades.

In the next session, two weeks later, November 2009, the conversation began with my good feelings about having discovered the primary source of my deep sadness and the mistaken childhood belief that I was unwanted. A recollection had occurred to me a few days before this session. It happened during my internship year in 1961-62 when I had my first taste of alcohol and accepted a bourbon and water at someone's home. I was twenty-four years old. My clear desire at the time was to be able to feel as socially acceptable as others in a group accustomed to social drinking. That event was the beginning of my long entanglement with alcohol, which became an addiction lasting nearly twenty-six years until early 1987.

Our discussion turned to attitudes toward alcohol in my family. Alcohol use was frowned upon among both my parents and all of my grandparents. In fact, my father's mother was an active member of the Women's Christian Temperance Union, commonly known as the WCTU. And on several occasions, I heard my Dad refer to alcoholic beverages as "John Barleycorn," the title of a Robert Burns poem. It was intended as a disparaging term.

I asked Dr. A. about the comment she had made in the previous session about wanting to teach me some meditation techniques. She had forgotten to bring the timer she uses in her own mediation times. Nevertheless, we could still cover some introductory approaches. Not long after she began to offer her suggestions, I asked her to stop.

"I need to be quiet. I need to feel control." I sat quietly, wordless.

"What's happening? What are you feeling.?"

I wasn't sure, but as I sat, the sadness began to creep back.

"It's about Mom. The hurt is back. It's about 'she doesn't want me.'"

Dr. A. asked me to talk to Mom, as if she was sitting in the chair right there. It was hard. At first, I didn't want to do it, but then relented.

"Mom, it hurts. It feels like you don't want me. I know it's not your fault. I can't touch you because your face hurts. But it hurts me. I love you, but I can't touch you."

The pain was real. Painful, breath-taking tears again came from deep inside. My question to Dr. A:

"Why does it hurt so much?"

She said: "Because this is real trauma. It is a lot like Post Traumatic Stress." She described what happens when little babies are not held and cradled and touched. "They wither and die. You were only six and a half. You couldn't understand what was happening. Children have magical thinking. They can easily believe that when something bad happens it's their fault."

I told her about getting my big, brown teddy bear from the guest room earlier this week. It was where all the stuffed animals are kept for the grandkids. I needed to hug him. We ended the session understanding there surely was more to uncover. I asked for our next session to be in four weeks, after Thanksgiving.

When I got home, I got Bear again and simply sat hugging him for a while. He is my little boy self. He just needed to be hugged for a while to feel safe. Later that afternoon, I realized that I had been feeling badly, almost guilty, for having to tell Mom how hurt I felt when I couldn't touch her and couldn't be near her.

One of the critical aspects of this has been that it became important for me to begin to take care of my internal little boy, the person who, as a child, experienced loneliness and a deep yearning for warmth and caring. The hurt little boy who was called "Robin" as a child was not yet sure that the adult Rob was a person he could trust to care for him. Through the ensuing weeks of the therapy process, that trust would begin to grow stronger as the process of healing old emotional pathways continued.

Two days after the November session, I was daydreaming about the role play with Mom in which I told her how hurt I felt, believing she didn't want me. I began to play in my mind a reply from her. I imagined hearing her say to me: "I didn't know how hurt you were. I do love you. I didn't mean to hurt you. Mommy got sick, but that's not your fault."

When I saw Dr. A. in December, I wasn't sure why I was feeling anxious. I recalled the previous session in which I expressed to Mom my feelings of rejection. Now, in the current session I was not liking the thought of expressing unhappiness with my Mom about repressed feelings of rejection from the time of her illness. I don't like having the feeling that I have not been kind to others in my relationships.

Dr. A. wondered if I had feelings of anger toward Mom. I couldn't say that I had felt anger, but I regretted that I wasn't able to know about the feelings of rejection from childhood much sooner, and been able to work through them with her before she died. Because that didn't happen and perhaps could not have happened, a gap was created between us which was never bridged. I'm left feeling I was cheated out of warmth and a depth of relationship other kids had. One of my vivid memories from my junior high years is visiting the home of a classmate. Seeing her interact with her mom with a warm hug and visible love made me yearn for the same feelings with my Mom.

Near the end of this session, I referred to the fact that one of my fantasies is that I could one day feel again the way I did in the days when I was in seminary when I looked forward to new experiences, and thoroughly enjoyed my work. Especially in the first two years, life was full of purposefulness. Dr. A.'s response was to assure me that getting to such a place is what this process is all about.

Later, in a conversation with my wife, I described the experience of observing my friend's relationship with her Mom, and mentioned the therapist's asking if I felt anger toward Mom. I said, "Not that I could find. It was more a case of resentment."

In the last session for 2009, I brought up Ginny's and my conversation. Dr. A. pushed me to describe how I explained to myself why I didn't have warm feelings toward my Mom. "How did you explain to yourself the lack of warmth – what did you tell yourself?" She alluded again to the possibility of anger or resentment. I could connect with resentment. I said: *"She was sick. She was broken."* Suddenly the tears came, and again the awful pain. *"My Mom was broken. She died."* (meaning emotionally). *"That's why she couldn't relate to me. That's why Dad did so many things that normally a Mom would do."* As the tears subsided, Dr. A. said: "Your Mom was very depressed. She never really recovered from her illness. And there were not the psychiatric resources available sixty years ago which we have now."

Slowly, a realization came to me. I looked directly at Dr. A. and said: *"You knew this all along. You knew I was going to come upon this painful recognition, didn't you?"* She replied with a gentle "Yes." **What I had never allowed myself to believe was a painful truth: my mother never recovered the person she was before her illness** when Gregory was born in 1944. Writing it down again brings the tears all over again. The grieving still is not over. Perhaps some dimension of it will remain, a permanent testimony to what was lost.

In the night following this session (Dec. 18-19) I slept poorly, awakening twice and listlessly ruminating about what I had discovered. The next day, Saturday, turned out to be a very down day. A huge snowstorm had begun overnight. Snow fell all day Saturday until 10:00 P.M., leaving behind fourteen inches. Nothing moved on Sunday. Still listless and "down," I went out to shovel the driveway. The fresh air and exertion helped me feel better. Finally, the street in front of our house was plowed on Monday.

With the holidays coming, I would not have another session with Dr. A. until January 22, 2010. My journal entry for Dec. 28 reads in part: "I'm beginning to think I've about run the course on whatever there is to find out about this pain and sadness about Mom that has been buried in me for so long and now is uncovered." Almost in the same moment, these questions arose: "Will I have a day or two in every week when I don't feel like doing much of anything, for at least part of the day? If what I am experiencing really is like post-traumatic stress, what is it really going to take to get beyond it?"

The January session became a summing up of what I had discovered over four months of therapy. For several reasons, I needed to step back from therapy. Most importantly, I was feeling as if I wasn't ready to do any more work. Yes, I had framed some lingering questions. But there was so much we had already uncovered. I needed somehow to absorb it and try to learn to accept it as part of the truth of my life and that of my family.

As part of this session, I took with me a family portrait, probably taken in early 1947. I was very nearly ten years old. (photo at the end of the chapter). It is a stiff formal portrait. My father looks closed. I don't know how to read my mother, other than that she has aged remarkably, even though she is a few months short of 40 years old. Dr. A, looking at the photograph, could see on their faces the pain my parents could not hide. Gregory stands next to Mom, probably just a few weeks past age three. I am standing at the back of the group with Frank, almost seven and Alan, not quite five.

I believe the photo was taken either late in 1946 or in early 1947, before the family moved to Sandusky, Ohio. I don't know what motivated my parents to want a family photo taken in our home, unless it was to leave a photo with the congregation Dad was serving at the time. I had not ever had feelings about it one way or another until I happened onto it while going through a number of family photos after I was in therapy. When I saw it, I was struck with the visible stiffness of us, and especially the lack of emotion or feeling in my Dad. It confirmed my feeling, expressed to Dr. A., that I was missing warmth in my childhood.

At this stage in my therapeutic journey, I continued to feel the sadness that began at age six and a half and was buried for so long. I have begun to find ways to cope with what had been my mistaken belief and feeling that I was being rejected by Mom because I was not allowed to touch her face due to the lingering painful tingling left by her illness. My notes from January 22, 2011 continue:

> *"The realization has become clear that I now have to see my childhood and my family in a new way – no longer idealized. And I have to live through the grief over the hurts I experienced until I find acceptance of what my childhood was as well as acceptance of a new sense of myself."*

I still would have to explore my past much more deeply. This was becoming both a story of broken attachment with my Mom, and a story about the impact of her illness on us as a family. Before digging more deeply into the breadth of the story and its effects, it is important to understand the meaning of attachment and its centrality in the process of developing emotional well-being.

Article describing Mom's illness
and Greg's birth
Bridgeport Sunday Herald,
March 5, 1944

Baby's Born As Paralysis Is Conquered

By ETHEL BECKWITH

Some babies will take the hard way for getting born but this is a story of one who found he couldn't trick anybody at Bridgeport hospital.

He is the fourth son of the Rev. and Mrs. Robert F. R. Peters of Park st. Congregational church.

Although he was born Feb. 2, The Herald is first to announce that his 100% arrival marked an amazing feat in local medical history.

HIT BY PARALYSIS

The minister's wife was afflicted 10 days before the birth with a form of paralysis.

It is not infantile paralysis but a virus that affects the nerve-centers.

Mrs. Peters, when brought to the hospital, could scarcely move and was in acute pain because of

Continued on PAGE TWELVE

Baby's Born In Odd Case

Continued from PAGE ONE

this affliction.

Since anesthetic slows respiration, her doctor, Dr. Estella M. Strayer, faced a dilemma.

She called on Dr. William German, noted neurologist of New Haven, and Dr. Crawford Griswold, Bridgeport obstetrician.

Dr. German was leaving to join the navy. He was prevailed on to come to the local hospital for consultation with Drs. Strayer and Griswold.

Helpless and inert while her pain increased, the invalid didn't know that the decision was to make the delivery without any anesthetic, on the big chance that the baby at least would survive.

Dr. Strayer resolved to save both, had an iron lung ready for Mrs. Peters.

Beside it was an oxygen tent, while the Rev. Mr. Peters and two friends stood ready to offer transfusions.

The doctor kept telling Mrs. Peters, as she demanded anesthetic, "Any minute now—any minute," while the boy took his time—he was six hours arriving.

Precarious moments p a s s e d when it was not known whether either of the two lives involved could take it.

WEIGHS NINE POUNDS

Dr. Strayer was no less jubilant than the minister when the boy, who henceforth shall be Gregory Peters, presented his appearance, weighing nine pounds.

Rallying better than expected, Mrs. Peters did not require the iron lung but was placed at once under an oxygen tent where she received the three transfusions.

Still it was three or four days before it could be certain that the strain on the paralyzed body was within human endurance.

The story goes now into its happy-ending phase.

Mrs. Peters is literally learning to walk, using a "walker" such as supports the weak legs of children.

Slowly she is improving from the pre-birth illness, known as periradiculitis, or inflammation of the nerve-roots.

The children are being cared for by the mother of Mrs. Peters, who was formerly Mary Caris.

Naturally the pleased pastor is stirred to a sermon. "It proved to me," he says, "the essential goodness of people. But I can tell you it was terrifying."

As a friend of the family, Dr. Strayer presents him with both his wife and baby as a present.

"We could never repay her," says the pastor.

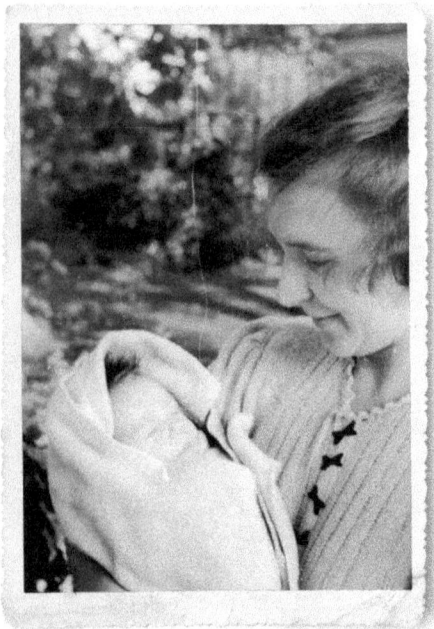

Me, at age six plus, on the steps of
Park Street Congregational Church

Mom holding me at one month old

Gregory, Alan, Frank and Rob enjoy a lunch stop in eastern
Pennsylvania during the family trip in August, 1946 from
Bridgeport to grandparents Caris' home in Ohio

My family, early 1947, L. to R. Alan (age 4), Mom, Gregory seated (2),
Rob (10), Dad, and Frank (7)

Park Street Congregational Church, Bridgeport, Connecticut

Chapter 2

Attachment:
A Critical Factor for Every Child

BEFORE I MET PROFESSOR FRANK STALFA, THE WORD ATTACHMENT MEANT LITTLE TO ME, OTHER THAN AN ADDENDUM ATTACHED TO SOMETHING ELSE. Frank Stalfa was a pastor, trained therapist and member of the faculty at Lancaster Theological Seminary. He was one of the primary professors in my Doctor of Ministry program, work I completed between September 1995 and May 1998. Sadly, Professor Stalfa was struck down by cancer in the middle of his career, thus depriving a generation of students the benefit of his teaching. He was especially interested in factors in a person's family of origin which most significantly influenced decisions related to one's choice of career. His concern was directed to individuals who choose careers in the helping professions, for example: ministry, social work, and counseling. His research explored such issues as: "In what ways are students' career plans influenced by parents?" "To what extent did such factors overlook a student's primary skills or personal interests?" "Were there significant events within a family's history which impacted career choices?" My family story is a significant example of the concern which was the focus of Professor Stalfa's research.

The first time I heard the word "attachment" used as a term in psychology was in 1996 during Professor Stalfa's course on the pastoral care of individuals facing grief and loss. A key topic in the course addressed the psychological foundations and dynamics of how and why each of us grieves our losses. This was a new topic for me. I had never considered theories in psychology which might explain deep feelings of grief and mourning, following a major loss, whether of a beloved person or of a job, or even a treasured object. The theory of attachment was a revelation. It describes how each of us relates in the very early weeks and months of our lives to our mother or the person who is our primary caregiver. Our early attachment, as well as our attachments later in life, play an important role in our future experiences of grieving.

The class took place more than twenty years after my ordination. It was my first introduction to the fundamental psychological dynamic addressed by the theory of attachment. Attachment begins in the very first weeks of life and continues through the years of our childhood. It also is the fundamental dynamic behind the experience of grief and mourning because the loss of a beloved person breaks the bond of attachment that existed with the now-lost person. Attachment is not limited to the relationship between infants and caregivers, but also involves our human connections with significant others throughout our lives.

The course gave me an entirely new perspective for understanding the pain experienced by grieving people. It identified broken attachment as a fundamental dynamic in experiencing grief. It also offered new perspectives on ways in which funerals and memorial services can include practices which help address this intense human experience.

First Proponent of Attachment Theory

The theories about attachment in infants were developed in the years after the Second World War when English psychiatrist John Bowlby began to study babies in a London orphanage. He noticed that, in spite of having basic needs met (food, shelter and medical care), some babies failed to thrive. Among other realities, he observed that those babies in the orphanage nearest to the nurses' station were rocked and cuddled more frequently than those farther away. The babies farthest away from the nurses appeared not to thrive as well as the others. Bowlby's research into the phenomenon led to his seminal ideas and formulation of the theory of childhood attachment. His book, *Attachment*, published in 1969, was the first volume in a three-volume study titled *Attachment and Loss*. Two additional books in the trilogy explored *Separation and Anxiety* and *Loss (1)*.

Bowlby provided significant new insights about how children first develop emotions which are foundational to psychological health throughout life. He described the sequence in which these emotions and reactions are established by growing infants. Bowlby's theory of attachment shed new light on how it is that human babies develop strong connections to adults, particularly to the one who is the primary source of care, food and safety. Bowlby provided a new understanding of how children first develop the emotions which are foundational to psychological health throughout life. Attachment theory posits that babies begin to be attuned at a very early age to seek a reliable caregiver, usually the mother, who is nearby and will be a source of safety and nurture. In the early weeks of life, babies begin to distinguish between reliable sources of comfort and care and sources which represent discomfort or even threat. Over the long span of human existence, babies have developed the innate strategies for seeking a caregiver on which they can rely for their safety, nourishment and nurture.

Bowlby illuminated the causes behind the intense disturbances, such as crying and anger, which occur when an infant is unexpectedly separated from his/her primary care giver, most often the mother. His work offered me a way of understanding how a child's unexpected separation from its mother can trigger anger as well as depression and emotional separation from its parent. **For me, the disruption of my connection to my mother led to long-lasting negative effects on my emotional development and contributed to the stresses later in my life. The details will emerge as the story unfolds.**

Numerous research studies since Bowlby have contributed to increased knowledge about the complexities of attachment. Among the important findings are the primary "styles" of attachment. The most desirable style that infants need to develop is termed "secure" attachment. This occurs when the primary caregiver, usually the mother, responds attentively to the infant's needs. It learns first that she is reliably available, and second that she is a source of safety and comfort. Adults whose childhood attachments were secure are able to rely on other people and to form close relationships.

Several additional attachment styles have been noted. One is "anxious" attachment, a variation in which an infant is "uneasy" and is guarded or uncertain about what responses it may receive from its mother. As adults, those who have experienced "anxious" attachment likely will find it difficult to be close to others and may doubt that they are loveable.

A third style is termed "avoidant" attachment. It occurs when infants and toddlers are left largely to care for themselves. Their cries indicating needs often go unheeded, and as adults they tend not to depend on others. They also tend to think they can take care of things without the aid of others. These are people likely to avoid emotions when a major loss happens. A fourth style is termed "disorganized" and involves long-term effects which include a desire to be close to others, alternating with fears of rejection and efforts to push people away.

The Role of the Brain

In my years in therapy, it has been important to become familiar with the ways in which the brain produces and records emotions. Two parts of the brain are particularly important to understanding how emotions are developed and communicated by the brain. Interestingly, the components which govern emotions develop much earlier than the parts which produce thinking and rationality (2).

The amygdala is the center for retaining emotions and the memory of emotional events. It is the place from which my many experiences of tears and recalled emotional pain came. When infants are held and stroked and comforted, these actions send messages of soothing to the brain. These have the effect of stopping the racking sobs of an infant. Creatures without an amygdala do not feel emotions such as joy or sadness.

A second portion of the brain is the source of thinking and enables us to put together and understand what our senses perceive. The addition of this part of the brain, the neocortex, makes possible the bond between mother and baby, or the primary caregiver and the baby. Without this part of the brain, which enables a mother's ability to establish affection and a critical bond with her infant, close family connections are not possible. Thus, when the mother-child bond is interrupted in some way in early life, permanent negative changes can occur in the character of family relationships.

EFFECTS OF NEGATIVE ATTACHMENTS

When secure attachment is interrupted by a change in an infant's feelings of security, or the infant senses that its once-secure caregiver is no longer available so that the source of its care becomes unpredictable, then specific and known changes begin to occur in the brain. When separated from its primary caregiver, the infant senses its safety is at risk, and it experiences a dramatic increase in the release of stress hormones which regulate the brain's fight or flight response. Young children who are five and six years of age can also experience these changes in the brain if they encounter an interruption of what had been a secure relationship. This is true when the bond is broken by an unexpected separation from the mother as can happen in the sudden absence of the mother through illness or death. I was six and a half when my mother became ill.

Both of my therapists believe that it was likely that during my infancy and earliest years I did experience secure attachment with my mother. (See the photo with her.) However, the disruption caused by her seven weeks of absence during her illness substantially altered my relationship with her. My emotional belief that "Mommy doesn't want me anymore" is an obvious clue, pointing to the significant traumatic change in my sense of security. Moreover, the changes in her attentiveness and emotional availability which occurred after she came home also contributed to my distress.

The literature about attachment affirms that a particular person's attachment style and its characteristics can be identified with the help of a psychologist especially trained in administering what is known as the Adult Attachment Interview. I have not participated in this interview. My sense of things is that Mom's absence caused a change in the nature of my attachment relationship. It introduced experiences of anxiety, or at least uncertainty, with which I coped as best I could.

Mom's illness occurred when I was at the age psychologists know to be a time when a child is prone to what is known as "magical thinking," namely a tendency for a child to blame itself as the cause when something bad takes place in its world. While I do not have the sense that I blamed my mother for being absent – it was not her fault that she became ill – I am keenly aware that after she returned home, I did not feel great warmth and affection for her. It is difficult to acknowledge that this was so. I want to be clear. I recognize that, as she slowly recovered from the aftereffects of her illness, she fulfilled many of the tasks of supporting a family of four young boys while Dad dealt with his duties as the lone full-time pastor to a large congregation. At the same time, it became his role to take on many support activities, including all of the grocery shopping. After her illness, Mom rarely drove the car.

In her later years, after she and Dad moved to a retirement community, Mom became a volunteer at the front welcome desk of the nursing home in their community. On the occasions when I visited, I often heard residents tell me how warm and welcoming she was as she received visitors and directed them to various patient's rooms. The complements sounded strange to me. Numerous people shared expressions of appreciation of her to me, and I am sure they **did** experience a genuine warmth from her. They and she were in a different setting from those in which I related to her. Their comments about her warmth to others came to me years before my journey in therapy. My brain had not yet had an opportunity to rewire, if I may use the term, the neural pathways which still remembered the childhood sense of rejection and the feelings of emotional distance.

LOSS AND GRIEVING

The theory of attachment recognizes that an infant or young child who senses that the mother is absent, or that the secure bond is lost or altered, will make efforts to restore it. The risk of losing the bond creates significant stress in the child.

Bowlby wrote extensively about the experience and effects of loss and grieving which occurs when the bond with the mother is broken. If a child senses the bonds will be lost, strong responses such as crying, hanging on to mother, or becoming angry at the thought of the mother leaving occur. Such intense behavior comes to an end if the mother does not leave and the threat of loss is removed. While the risk of loss of connections with my mother may have been reduced by the possibility that my father explained the reason for my mother's absence, her loss during seven weeks of her hospitalization still had a significant impact on my emotions. In my own experience, the grieving was repressed, and when my mother's return occurred, my bonds with her were never fully restored. Did I unconsciously worry that she might leave again? Clearly, something caused me to believe, mistakenly, that she did not want me anymore. However, in order to survive emotionally, I never let the long-buried feeling surface. In addition to repressing the thought, I buried my deep grief over the loss of an emotionally warm connection. These changes in emotional well-being led to behaviors later in my life which were destructive to my well-being.

Bowlby describes outcomes which may occur if attachment is not restored. The intense reactions may occur with less frequency, but they do not disappear, and the feelings of loss can continue to recur. In the case of permanent loss of the mother through death or other circumstance, the response is likely to be one of profound grief and mourning.

A parenthetical comment: I must note that this chapter is being written in 2018 just when the tragedy of the federal government's separation of children from their asylum-seeking parents has been exposed. The long-term negative impact on the separated children has been decried by the vast majority of medical and mental health professionals. My own experience underscores their alarm. **These children will suffer psychological and health disturbances of varying degrees of intensity, and much of their effects will be repressed long into the future, causing emotional issues for years, and for many individuals, decades after the separation occurred.**

In my own life, the factual story of my mother's illness and absence from the family was never forgotten. The feelings of distance from Mom, and the sense that she didn't want me any more went unrecognized by my parents and the adults who knew me. Much later in therapy, I learned that when a child's emotions and feelings go unrecognized, the psychological trauma which results can be as harmful as physical or verbal abuse. The change in the attachment relationship alters the way the person relates to others and the wider world. This is why my primary therapist explained that my reaction to Mom's illness and absence truly was trauma. It was a key factor in shaping how I functioned in my youth and the early years of my career. The residual effect of the traumatic experience influenced the choices I made and facilitated making decisions which were harmful to me and hurtful to others.

This therapeutic journey has helped me recognize that, in spite of my efforts to achieve warmer interactions with her, Mom really was not capable of overcoming the un-recognized aftereffect which caused her to be emotionally unavailable. This is a source of sadness for me. I now see that my Mom may have experienced a level of depression following her illness which contributed to her emotional distance, but did not completely overwhelm her. While I mourn the affectionate Mom who was not available to me, I appreciate what she was able to provide in terms of her support of my school work and activities. Understanding my altered attachment relations provides an essential piece of the context for the rest of the story. I explore next the outlines of my life and choices I made.

Notes

1. Bowlby, John, *Loss: Sadness and Depression, Vol. III* of *Attachment and Loss*, (New York, Basic Books, second edition, 1982, 10th Anniversary Edition 2006).

2. Goleman, Daniel, *Emotional Intelligence, Why It Can Matter More Than IQ*, (New York, Bantam Books, 2005).

3. Lovenheim, Peter, *The Attachment Effect*, (New York, Penguin/ Random House, 2018).

Chapter 3

Family Story

MY HERITAGE IS ROOTED IN TWO GENERATIONS OF ORDAINED MINISTERS ON MY MOTHER'S SIDE OF THE FAMILY AND SIX GENERATIONS OF PREACHERS AND ORDAINED MINISTERS ON MY FATHER'S SIDE. Many of my female relatives were teachers, and grandfather Caris's two brothers were mathematics professors. My three brothers and I were nurtured in an atmosphere of commitment to religious faith and regular church attendance. My parents and grandparents respected the professions and were deeply connected to the early years of Ohio's history. They cared about, and passed on to us, similar expectations along with their families' stories. It was assumed we would earn college degrees and pursue professional careers.

During the grade school and junior high school years, after the family moved to Sandusky in 1947, I gradually became aware of the family's background. Mom and Dad grew up in Defiance, Ohio. My mother was born there on July 21, 1907, the first of six living children. A sister died of scarlet fever as a very young child. I never learned her name. Mom attended elementary, junior and senior high school in Defiance. She was valedictorian of her high school class. She was graduated from Defiance College in June, 1925, also as valedictorian.

Her parents were prominent in Defiance. Her father, Albert Garfield Caris, was born on September 13, 1881 near Cardington, Ohio, the son of Elder Squire A. Caris, (Born July 3, 1851). The term "Elder" was the equivalent of the more modern "Reverend." He was a minister in the Christian denomination, also known as the Christian Connection. The Christian Connection came into being in the late 18th century and came to be known as the Christian Church. It merged with the Congregational Churches in 1931, which became part of the new United Church of Christ in 1957.

Grandfather Caris graduated from high school in Watkins, Ohio in

1896, and after some study at Ohio Wesleyan College, received the A.B. degree at Defiance College in 1907. He began teaching in the commercial department in 1907. In 1908, he became head of the mathematics department at Defiance. Through the years he rose to become Dean of the College and then President, a role he filled from 1919 through June 1931. He married Gertrude Jennings in 1904. He was ordained a minister by the Ohio Central Christian Conference in 1908 and was awarded the honorary Doctor of Letters degree in 1914 by Elon College in North Carolina. Elon was one of the institutions associated with the Christian denomination.

My clearest memories of grandmother Caris date from when I was ten years old, and our family moved from Connecticut to Ohio. By then, they were in their late sixties. Grandmother Caris was active in the nearby Methodist church. I recall visiting in the summer, when the family would spend several vacation days at our grandparents' home in late August. It was a small three-bedroom house in New Rome, a small town on U.S. Route 40 west of Columbus, where they moved after World War II. Grandmother Caris would send us boys out to gather the apples that fell from the tree in the backyard so she could make applesauce. The house would fill with aroma of cooked apples. She mashed them a metal colander to separate the cooked apple pulp from the skins. Every year, she made several dozen jars of sweet, seasoned applesauce. Some of it was always part of the Thanksgiving meal. Some of it would end up at the church's food booth at the fair in Hilliard, not far from New Rome. My first experience seeing 4-H youth projects in raising prize cattle and hogs happened at the Hilliard Fair.

I will always remember Grandfather Caris's big, mission-style rocking chair which he occupied whenever he was relaxing. Saturday afternoons were often spent sitting in that chair, listening to WBNS and the broadcast of the Ohio State Buckeyes football game. He was fond of teaching us new words. One of his favorite lessons was to teach us the longest word in English, antidisestablishmentarianism. And he could tell wonderful stories about his childhood and youth working on a family farm in the late 1890s, in the days before there were electric lights.

The Peters name was also well known in Defiance. Dad was born on June 30, 1908 in Coshocton in Morrow County, Ohio. He was one of three sons born to the Rev. Frank H. Peters and Sadie Watson Peters. Dad's brother, Ralph, was twelve years older, and a third son, born after Ralph, died in infancy. Uncle Ralph became prominent in Defiance and northern Ohio. He was the publisher of the *Defiance Crescent News* for many years, and later served at the Director of the Maumee Water Conservancy District.

Grandfather Peters was born April 3, 1872 in Frazeysburg, Ohio and ordained in the Christian church in 1893. He served in several communities, including New Bedford and Fall River, Massachusetts and Yellow Springs, Ohio before moving to Defiance in 1919 to become the minister of the College Christian Church on the Defiance College campus. He served on the board of trustees of the college for several years. He was a member of the board of directors of Franklinton Academy in Bricks, North Carolina. This was a school for African American students located near Elon College. In 1929, he was called to First Congregational Church in Strongsville, Ohio and served nearly eighteen years, retiring in 1947. He and his wife returned to the home they owned on Nicholas Street in Defiance. This was the house Dad knew in his teen and college years.

We made a visit to Dad's parents' home in Strongsville, Ohio sometime near the end of World War II, perhaps a couple of years before they retired. Grandma Peters was still canning vegetables from their sizeable garden. Every year she "put up," as the expression was, more than two hundred quart-size jars of vegetables as a major source of their winter food supply. There also were jars of canned chicken meat. It came from chickens no longer laying eggs culled from the flock of chickens they kept. Dad's parents knew what it was to provide for themselves because they lived through the Great Depression when there was very little money from a meager minister's salary (often less than $100 a month). My memory of Grandma Peters is of a fairly large, older woman wearing her kitchen apron, baking wonderful apple and pumpkin pies for Sunday dinner.

For reasons I cannot fully explain, I developed a great fondness for

Grandpa Peters. He liked to play a favorite game with me. On more than one occasion, when visiting the house in Defiance, the following event would take place. When it was nearly lunch time, Grandma would realize that she didn't have enough milk in the house for the four of us boys. She would ask Grandpa to go to the dairy store for milk. In turn, Grandpa asked me if I wanted to go along. I answered: "Sure," and he would say: "Maybe we'll go over to Fort Wayne while we're out." And so, we would get in his old Ford coupe, and head to the Arps Dairy store downtown. Grandpa would go in and get the milk. When he returned to the car, I would ask: "Are we going to Fort Wayne now?" He usually replied, "We'll, I guess Grandma wants us home for lunch, so we'd better go back with the milk." We never did go to Fort Wayne in his old Ford coupe.

As far as I know, Grandpa Peters' only theological training was gained by "reading for the ministry." This involved reading the Christian denomination's prescribed bibliography under the guidance of an experienced pastor over a period of three years. The candidate was subjected to periodic oral examinations. To receive ordination, the candidate was interviewed and recommended for ordination by the denomination's committee on the ministry. The committee included representatives from neighboring Christian churches.

Dad attended public schools in Defiance and was graduated from Defiance College in 1929, the same year as Mom. She taught school in Swanton, Ohio for two years while Dad completed his first two years of seminary. He and Mom were married on June 12, 1931 and then returned to New Haven and Yale Divinity School for Dad's final year. Their wedding ceremony was held in the garden of the president's house at Defiance College and performed by Dad's father. Eighteen days later, Grandfather Caris's resignation from the presidency became effective, and the family had to move from the campus. He had submitted his resignation in January of 1931 to be effective at the end of the academic year. Sometime in my teen years, I learned of his resignation. However, Mom and Dad never spoke of the reason for his leaving and seemed reluctant to talk about it.

Recently I discovered, through research in Defiance, that he decided to resign largely because of the financial challenges to the College resulting from the Great Depression. These issues caused significant discord about how to address them, and apparently led him to his decision. It had to be a difficult choice because the family would have to relocate, and Grandpa was faced with finding a job in a depressed economy. Ultimately, after a relatively brief time with the John Hancock Insurance Company, he became the head statistician in the State of Ohio office which regulated insurance companies. He retired after twenty years of service.

From an early age, my parents began sharing the stories of growing up in Defiance and the activities of their college years. Mom lived on the campus with her family in the president's house until she graduated from college. Among her many activities, she was an able athlete in tennis and basketball. She was a musician as well and was the accompanist for the Men's Glee Club. The 1928 picture of her reveals an attractive, young woman. She and her sister spent one summer waiting tables at the Christian denomination's conference center, Craigville, on Cape Cod. My brothers and I were well aware that she earned straight A grades, both in high school and college. We grew up with the expectation that we would maintain very good grades.

Dad lived with his parents at 718 Nicholas Street, only a block from the campus. He was a reporter for the campus paper and its editor at least one year. He edited the yearbook for 1929. He was a cheerleader, a member of the Men's Glee Club and a baritone soloist. He gave some thought to becoming a professional singer before settling on the ministry. He received a letter of introduction to the head of the vocal music department at Yale. I don't know whether he ever pursued voice training at Yale. He was awarded the honorary Doctor of Divinity degree during the Defiance College commencement in 1959. It was granted in recognition for his service to the United Church of Christ, the denomination with which Defiance College is loosely affiliated today.

There never was doubt that we boys would attend college and pursue significant careers. It is a testament to my parents' commitment to our educations that we found a way not only to achieve college degrees, but also earn Master's degrees as well. This was accomplished on a minister's salary, and Mother's occasional part-time substitute teaching and tutoring, as well as each of us having various summer jobs and newspaper delivery routes. All of us had to take out only limited loans to meet some expenses. In fact, I graduated from seminary owing just $500 to Yale University. In later years, my brothers needed to take larger loans, but they were far less than most present-day students incur.

THE ELEMENTARY SCHOOL YEARS

I have limited recollections of my very first years of schooling. In September of 1943, I attended Beardsley Park Elementary School in Bridgeport, Connecticut to start first grade. My one recollection is of the teacher helping us create a play store. We brought empty food product cartons to "sell" in our play store. It was a way to learn the uses of numbers. But in late October, needing a larger home because my youngest brother was expected the following January, we moved to Fairview Avenue. I transferred to Madison School. This was the first of several disruptions in my school experience.

MADISON SCHOOL IN BRIDGEPORT, CONNECTICUT

I remember several things about Madison School. One is the Flag Day celebration every year. It was held out-of-doors. The older students would line both sides of the long walkway leading to the front door of the school. Each student held a large American flag on a long flagpole. It was quite a sight to see dozens of American flags waving in the June breeze. The students all stood with the flags while a brief program was conducted. Dad enjoyed taking pictures of the event.

The second memory is of my third-grade teacher, whose name has long been repressed. One day, she caught me passing a note to a classmate during class and sent me to the coat room for a "timeout." I don't think it was called a "timeout" in those days. All I heard was "You can go to the coat room, young man." It seemed I spent an eternity in the semi-dark coat room, which was really a big closet next to the class room where all our coats were hung each day.

The third memory, from fourth grade, is having to take part in competitions for memorizing multiplication tables. The class stood around the edges of the room, and the teacher would point to a multiplication problem on the chart, (for example 12 x 8) and the next person in the line had to give the answer. If that student was wrong, he or she sat down. I usually wasn't the last one standing, the winner. No one wanted to be the first to sit. These drills always made me fearful I would be first one to sit out.

The fourth distinctive thing about Madison School was the early release on Wednesday afternoon so that we could attend mid-week church school class. I don't remember where it was held, and I know nothing of the public law that encouraged this sort of public support of religious education. I did not encounter this arrangement when we moved to Ohio.

One other lasting memory is of the Madison School playground where I first learned to play dodgeball at recess. It seemed that I was always the one to be stuck with being "it," and then it took me many attempts before succeeding at making somebody else "it." These weren't the only reasons I didn't like Madison, but they were enough to develop a dislike for school. In August of 1947, after fourth grade, our family moved to Sandusky, Ohio.

Monroe School in Sandusky

The first day of school in September of 1947 was a bright sunny day. For me it offered lots of uncertainty. I could not imagine on that day that the two short years I spent at Monroe School would provide me with the two best friends I ever had out of my grade school and high school years.

Monroe School, on Monroe Street in Sandusky, was a grand, two-story limestone building. Built in 1894, it featured beautiful, red sandstone half-circle arches over the first- floor windows. They provided a distinctive contrast with the classic gray of the limestone walls. The school was closed in 2006 but still stands today, serving as a charter school for children in kindergarten through fifth grade.

Even though there was a large entrance with steps leading through a high arched entry facing Monroe Street, we always entered from the side door on Franklin Street near the playground. Inside was a large, square, central space. At each corner, a doorway led to a classroom. A wide staircase with wood steps led to the second floor. The treads of the steps had been worn concave from the thousands of school kids' shoes tramping to and from classes. On my first day in September, the principal, Miss Ohlemacher, directed me to Mrs. Golden's fifth-grade classroom. It was on the second floor in the northeast corner of the building. The bright morning sun shining though the high, double-sash windows made this a bright, cheerful place. I will always be grateful to my teacher, Mrs. Golden, who found a way to create in me a desire to learn.

Every school day for two years, I walked to Monroe School from our house at 322 East Adams Street, a distance of about three and a half blocks. On days when I might be late to school, I could run out the kitchen door, across the vacant lot to Franklin Street and race the remaining three blocks to school. With luck, I would beat the tardy bell. I don't remember ever being late, but I sure came close several times!

One of the now-humorous memories from Mrs. Golden's classroom involves the time I got caught passing notes, again. This time it was to the cute girl in the next row, Barbara Merkle. The note was intercepted by Mrs. Golden. To my utter embarrassment, she opened the note, silently read it, and then proceeded to lecture the class about how there would be time enough in the future to show romantic interest in members of the opposite sex. She then returned to whatever her topic of the day was. Everyone was sufficiently petrified by the lecture to become tightlipped about the episode. Mrs. Golden succeeded in snuffing out our little flirtation. Of course, our lives diverged. Years later, during a high school reunion, we had a laugh about the day Mrs. Golden caught me passing notes.

The real story, however, is that Mrs. Golden was the teacher who succeeded in making learning a source of excitement. I don't know how she did it, but somehow, I caught on to the idea that learning new stuff was fun. Cursive writing, however, was another matter. Handwriting was taught using the Palmer Method. Every day we had to learn how to shape upper and lowercase letters in cursive writing and eventually to link the letters together so that each word was written in an uninterrupted series of strokes. Each student had special lined paper to be used to guide the size of the letters.

Every session began with making a row of upper case and then lowercase versions of the letter "o." Then we would practice the new letter for the day. Each letter was repeated and linked to the next in a single row across the page. The model shapes were all displayed on a large chart at the front of the room. Recently, I found my old grade-school reports in an envelope. At the beginning of the year, I got failing marks because my letters looked nothing like the examples we were to imitate. Finally, on the last report card of the year, I got a "much improved" compliment about my handwriting. One other thing stood out about fifth grade. We had competitions to see which student would be first to find an assigned word in the dictionary. I was never first or last. Bob Thom was always first, and everyone knew he was the quickest and brightest of our class.

Sixth Grade

Sixth grade at Monroe School had a special character all its own. Our teacher, Mrs. Stack, knew French. Every now and then she would teach us simple phrases. We learned *ferme la porte* (close the door), *ouvrez la porte* (open the door), *respondez sil vous plait* (please reply) and several more now lost to memory. Sixth grade also was the year the principal asked me to go to the third-grade room to help a left-handed student learn how to write pushing his pencil instead of crooking his hand and pulling the pencil. Our principle was a strict disciplinarian, but she also was the kind of person who bandaged scrapped knees and elbows suffered on the playground during recess.

One element of the grade school experience is now gone from the routine of public schools. Every morning, the principal made the day's announcements and led the pledge of allegiance. The pledge was followed by a brief prayer for the day, usually led by one of the Protestant clergy in town. I only recall that Protestant clergy offered this prayer. I'm sure the Roman Catholic kids had prayers at the parochial school. I don't recall ever hearing a rabbi being introduced to offer the morning prayer. Thinking about it now, this was the acceptable form of public religion in Sandusky, a different version from the practice in the Bridgeport schools.

Two Best Friends

The two best friends I made at Monroe School were Tom Ryan and Bob Snyder. Tom's Dad was a policeman in Sandusky, and Bob's dad had a butcher shop. We were friends through high school, although Tom's family moved to California after our sophomore year. Until then, we were in Boy Scouts together. Our troop met at the Congregational Church on Monday nights. Every week after the meeting, we would walk to Tom Ryan's house to watch *I Love Lucy*. The Ryans had one of the early TV sets with the small oval screen. The picture was only in black and white. Remember, this was in the early 1950s. Not many people had TV. Cable TV didn't exist. There were only three channels – the three networks – ABC, NBC and CBS. TV signals were received through a tall antenna mounted on a pole on the roof. The pole was strapped to the chimney. The signal came from a tall relay tower some distance away. Sometimes, a high building or natural obstruction blocked the signal from one of the stations, so that a particular household might only receive the signal from one or two of the stations.

Expectations

In junior high and high school, I struggled to bring home schoolwork which pleased Mom. She had been a straight A student and a teacher of English and Latin, and she knew math as well. When I brought home test papers which had mistaken answers on them, she often would say to me: "You knew the answer to that question. I'm surprised you missed it." Or she might ask: "What happened with this question?" or "Did you misunderstand it?" My parents never complained about my overall grade average, but I often got the feeling from my Mom that I was not quite measuring up to what she expected. Over time, these comments influenced much of my self-perception about whether my work and effort were good enough to be acceptable.

Preacher's Kid

Growing up as a preacher's kid means that, through no fault of your own, you join a small segment of the American populace who experience the years of youth in ways most others don't, except perhaps children of the military. PKs, as we are known, are often the bearers of certain expectations that may not be thrust upon other kids. PKs usually are expected to be models of decorum. When we are not, we hear about it at home, as in "What will people think if the minister's kids don't behave well toward one another?" And of course, we would never get into a confrontation with a parishioner's kid. We were expected to be well-behaved.

As in everything, there are exceptions. It was reported that on one Sunday before we arrived in Sandusky, the son of one of my Dad's predecessors renewed his battle with another kid in the youth choir. On that Sunday morning, he summarily threw a hymn book across the choir loft at his rival. I never did hear how his dad responded to the youngster's antics. It might be an apocryphal story, but probably not. I don't doubt it was relayed to me as a clear message about how not to behave.

I was the oldest child in a family of four rambunctious boys. In the pre-school years, we probably didn't cause much stir other than the annoyance of playing tag through the sanctuary after church while parishioners went through the post-service greeting line. As we learned early in life, this was frowned upon.

As a young child, I did develop a tendency to speak out at odd times. One Sunday, during the service at Park Street Congregational Church in Bridgeport, when I was about three years old, I was sitting at the back of the church with my Mom. Dad was preparing to perform a baptism. He announced the invitation to the parents to come forward and present their child. He said, in a firm voice, "Will the parents desiring the baptism of their child please come forward?" To which I loudly replied: "Okay Daddy!" Everyone knew who had spoken up.

Then there was the Sunday when I was in Junior High, and my best friend, Bob Snyder, and I got to horsing around in church. Bob brought a big padlock with him to Sunday school. He and I were sitting in the second row from the front, right below the pulpit, during the sermon. My Mom wasn't there for some reason. We were sitting alone. Bob fished the lock out of his pocket, and we started passing it back and forth, fiddling with the key trying to open it. All of a sudden, the lock crashed to the wooden floor. The sound echoed through the sanctuary like the explosion of a howitzer. Dad stopped the sermon and glared at us, looking sterner than ever in his clerical collar and black pastor's robe. To our dismay, he delivered, in very clear terms, the suggestion that if we couldn't sit still, we could leave. We shrank down in the pew and didn't make another sound for the rest of the hour. That episode pretty much ended my horseplay at unacceptable times.

Occasionally, errant behavior can be more serious. One incident involved one of my brothers. Early in his high school years, he and a couple of buddies from the football team decided one evening to go over to the amusement park on Cedar Point after it was closed for the season. Let's just say that they managed to get into the park illegally and got caught. That one ended when Dad accompanied my brother to the juvenile court to assist him in avoiding juvenile jail time. Yes, one of the hazards of being a PK was the temptation to rebel against what seemed at times to be overly rigid requirements. Sometimes, we willingly risked infractions of what we thought were oppressive rules of behavior.

I'll never forget the night when Mom got creative with the discipline. Dad had gone out of town. Dinner was over, and it was time for bed. We headed upstairs and got into our pajamas. Two of us slept in bunk beds in one bedroom and the younger two slept in beds in a second room. We got to horsing around, joking and laughing back and forth between bedrooms. Then we got into a pillow fight. Pretty soon, Mom had had enough, warning us to settle down or she would do something drastic. It was quiet for about three minutes, and the horseplay started again. This time, Mom marched us all down to the dining room, turned on the overhead light and proceeded to order us to start a fast walk in single file around the dining room table. After a couple of minutes, she upped the pace to a steady run. When we began panting, she asked if we had had enough. Of course we wanted no more, and we were marched off to bed, breathless and exhausted, but unscathed. Not a creature was heard stirring, not even an errant PK.

NEWSPAPER BOY

Sometime in the spring of 1950, my seventh-grade year, I got my first paper route carrying the local afternoon paper, the *Sandusky Register*. I was beginning to save money for college. The life of a newspaper carrier was a daily routine made unpredictable by changes in the weather and the moods of customers. When it was sunny, customers tended to be agreeable. When fall turned to winter, and the skies grew gray, moods also seemed to turn dark. I dreaded facing the rain or the cold. I delivered papers riding my bicycle with a bag of folded papers slung over my shoulder, steering with one hand and pitching the papers with the other. New-fallen snow made slow going and presented the risk of losing control on a slippery hill or un-cleared sidewalk. In town, there were sidewalks on both sides of every street.

The moodiest days were Saturdays. On those mornings, it was necessary to go to each customer's front door to collect the money owed for the papers delivered the previous week. There was a system for collecting the payments. Every carrier had a large, metal, hinged ring which carried a record card for each customer. Each card was imprinted with the dates for fifty-two Saturdays. When a customer paid the bill, I punched the appropriate date on both my card and the customer's copy.

Saturday mornings became the opportunity, not always appreciated, for learning about the diverse temperaments of a wide variety of individuals. Some were sleepy-eyed, even at mid-morning. Some were cheerful and welcoming. Occasionally, I ran into a grump, especially if I had been unlucky enough to have forgotten a stop and the unhappy customer had to call, asking what had happened to a missing paper. Once in a while, a customer postponed payment, saying he or she didn't have change, or some other excuse.

Sometimes, with older, forgetful people, I would have to prove my case by comparing my punch card with the customer's copy.

Our profit amounted to two or three cents per paper. With about thirty customers, I would make around four dollars a week. But those were the days when a candy bar cost a nickel! In a year, I saved most of $150 from the *Sandusky Register* route. This sum was swelled by about $25 or $30 in Christmas tips that customers handed me when I did my collections in December.

I remember the neighborhood bar at the corner of Meigs and Jefferson. I delivered the afternoon *Sandusky Register* there. The bar had a wood floor that exuded a heavy aroma from many years' worth of spilled beer. It was all I could do not to hold my nose when I had to go inside on Saturdays to collect the weekly payment.

I carried the afternoon *Register* five days a week for a year before I also signed on in the Summer of 1951 to deliver the *Cleveland Plain Dealer*. The *Plain Dealer* was a morning paper. As September approached that year, I gave the afternoon route to my brother Frank. This would allow me to participate in after school activities when I started high school. From then on, I carried the *Plain Dealer* six days a week and Sunday morning for three years.

Dad became the hero of my newspaper business. On Sunday, my route was swelled by the Sunday-only customers to almost twice my thirty-four daily customers. The only way to carry the big load of heavy Sunday *Plain Dealer* papers was by car. We stacked the front seat and two thirds of the back seat full with about fifty papers. Dad drove, and I rode in the back seat so I could grab papers easily. They were delivered as I walked door-to-door, making sure the paper was out of the weather, under the doormat or inside a storm door to prevent being blown by the wind. We didn't have the plastic bags in use today.

My newspaper route taught me frugality. I had a large goal, helping to pay for college. I hated to spend money except in those moments when my sweet tooth couldn't resist the price of a candy bar. In hindsight, candy bars may have been a way of trying to feel good in contrast to the repressed feelings of hurt. And I learned that, with a very few exceptions, people are friendly and supportive. It is the rare person who seems to have been born grumpy, at least when dealing with the paperboy.

LIVING WITH THE FEELINGS

Depending on the situation, being a PK was a source of difficult feelings and emotions. One of the most difficult for me was enduring being treated as if I was always a "nice" boy because my father was a minister. From time to time, I would hear such remarks as "He doesn't cuss. His Dad is a minister." Such comments made me feel as if I was different from other kids. It was a feeling that somehow, I had to follow a different set of rules. That also was the feeling I got when the family visited the Peters grandparents. If it was on a Sunday afternoon, we were not allowed to throw a baseball. We knew that there were other rules that would have applied had we been older, strictures against card playing and dancing for example. We knew Dad had grown up under a strict regimen based on some very conservative religious views. At home, we boys did not face such rules.

When we moved to Sandusky, the two years at Monroe School were difficult because I had not grown up with the kids from the neighborhood. I got teased about my childhood nickname, "Robin," the name my parents called me to distinguish me from my Dad. Mom called him Bob, and they didn't want me to be known as Bobby. Kids who teased and called me such things as "Little Robin Red Breast" and "Tweet-Tweet." I pretty much felt like an outsider most of the time in those two years. Because I was not particularly athletic and was relatively small, I frequently was the last one chosen for playground games. I tended to feel embarrassed at such times.

There was, however, an episode which brought some respect. The neighborhood bully, John Souter, was a source of confrontation from time to time. In sixth grade, he started a rumor that he was going to beat me up after school. Word got around, and soon kids were asking me what I was going to do about it. They wondered if I was going to face off with him. Since we both walked the same route to school, the confrontation was inevitable. One day, the word was out that he was going to confront me.

That afternoon on the way home, I could see a bigger-than-usual cluster of kids hanging around at the end of the next block where there was a small triangle of vacant ground. It was created by a diagonal cross street. Seeing the knot of kids, I knew what would happen. It was unavoidable. When I got there, the now-growing cluster moved apart. John was waiting, glaring and threatening. I decided I had to give it everything I had. After circling each other for almost no time at all, we were in a knock-down, drag-out wrestling match on a dusty, grass-free patch of ground a block from the school. Each of us was trying desperately to overpower the other.

I was just about to pin John on his back, when a big voice burst through the ring of kids watching us tussle. I heard him say: "You two boys cut it out right now!" It was my father. He happened by in his car, saw what was happening, and stopped to break it up. It was only after he stepped through the quickly-scattering onlookers that he realized it was his son in the scuffle.

I was mad! Just on the brink of victory, my Dad had broken up my moment of glory. I know he was acting out of his adult perspective about kids not fighting. Even so, for a long time, I resented his interference. But enough was accomplished to protect my pride. Thereafter, John chose to ignore me.

But Dad's interruption also was another example of something he often had made clear at home. He would not tolerate harsh or physical conflict among us boys. When we were older, and had occasion to reminisce about our growing up, we each knew of times when Dad had intimated that, as a young person, he had experienced unpleasant conflict in his own home. We sensed he felt a need to ensure there was not any conflict in his home. In fact, he did not allow expressions of anger, and we did not learn positive ways to resolve conflicts until many years into adulthood.

Summer in Sandusky offered many attractions to occupy the attention of a young boy. During my junior high years, Dad bought a second-hand bicycle as a surprise birthday present for me. We carefully restored it. I remember we painted it gray, with a forest green stripe the length of each fender. It had balloon tires and wide handlebars. As kids, we rode our bikes everywhere. One summer day Tommy Fronizer and I packed sandwiches for lunch and rode six miles west of Sandusky to the little town of Castalia. Its notable feature was a tourist-attraction. It is a "bottomless" spring known as The Blue Hole.

A Summer Ride to the Greatest Amusement Park

However, some trips were not on our bikes. One was the boat ride to Cedar Point, an amusement park with the same name as the sandy spit of land which jutted out into Lake Erie and helped to form Sandusky Bay. Local tradition said it was once covered with cedar trees. In the 19th and 20th Centuries, a two-lane road and houses were built along the spit, facing the lake. The area was known as the "chaussee," a German and French word which originally meant "metal road." Early settlers of Sandusky were German, thus the name of this populated spit of land. I never knew whether the first road on it was actually metal.

The primary attraction of Cedar Point, other than the spectacular panorama of Lake Erie, was the amusement park at its tip. In the early 20th Century, its biggest promoter and developer was George A. Boeckling. In 1907, he became the general manager of the Cedar Point Gardens and Amusement Park. He expanded the gardens, added rides and built the wood structure of the Cyclone roller coaster. He also built a large summer hotel called The Breakers. There were picnic areas and bath houses for folks who wanted to swim in the lake. Today, Cedar Point is a greatly expanded amusement park. Its fans like to claim it is the "roller coaster capital of the world." It is reported to offer seventeen roller coasters.

From 1909 until 1951, the easiest, most direct way to get to Cedar Point was on the side-wheel river boat that sailed from the city pier at the foot of Columbus Avenue in downtown Sandusky. It was eight city blocks from our house on Adams Street to the pier where the G. A. Boeckling, a side-wheel ferry, named for the first developer of "The Point," was docked.

It sailed every hour on the hour across the bay to "the Point," and it returned on the half hour. A ride on the ferry cost about two bits, our slang for twenty-five cents.

The Boeckling had a paddle wheel amidships on the port and starboard sides. She was known as a "double-ender." She was rounded at each end to fit into a ferry slip and had a pilot house on both ends. All the skipper had to do at the end of a run was walk to the opposite pilot house and reverse the rotation of the paddle wheels to begin the next run. The Boeckling was built with two decks. She had a large, comfortable interior cabin on each deck. A grand staircase led to the second deck. Both decks offered wide exterior promenades where passengers could enjoy warm summer breezes during the trip of two miles across the bay.

Occasionally, on a sunny summer day, we could pack a lunchbox, walk to the ferry and ride to Cedar Point. We'd walk around the amusement park, and if we had a little extra money, we might ride the bumper cars or buy some cotton candy. Usually we went for a swim in the lake before it was time to ride the ferry back across the bay. We always made sure to leave in time to be home before supper. Our parents were willing to let us go to "the Point" as long as they knew who we were with and when we would be home.

The Boeckling went out of service in 1951, replaced by other boats. In 1952, she was towed to Sturgeon Bay, Wisconsin and became a floating warehouse. In 1982, a preservation group bought her and had her towed 550 miles back to Sandusky. A fund-raising campaign was begun. In 1985, during a high school reunion, I visited the old boat, now a tired, down-at-the-heels shadow of her former glory. Eventually she was towed to Toledo for overhaul. While restoration was underway, a fire burned the superstructure to the waterline. Now a wreck, the restoration was abandoned and the hulk cut up for scrap.

You can find pictures of the G.A. Boeckling on the internet by entering her name. I still have the souvenir tee-shirt purchased during the reunion visit in 1985.

SOME SIDE BENEFITS TO BEING A PK

Despite being mischievous on occasion, we were the beneficiaries of great kindnesses from church folk. For example, in the 1950s, several families had summer cottages on the shores of Lake Erie. In those days, the lake was still a wonderful freshwater resource which offered a delightful escape from the un-air-conditioned mugginess of our house. We frequently were invited to spend a Sunday afternoon at the summer cottage of one parishioner or another at Hartley Beach. Often these outings ended with a casual picnic supper with our hosts before we headed home in the twilight of the summer evening.

I especially appreciated several kindnesses from church members when I was planning to spend my junior year of college at Silliman University in the Philippines. Perhaps the greatest for me was the willingness of two individuals, along with a fellowship group, to make loans and gifts that helped finance my special year. In fact, one of the loans was forgiven after I returned and gave illustrated presentations about what I had learned of Philippine life and culture.

I left parish ministry when my sons were very young, and they did not grow up being known up as PKs. They were still toddlers when I left parish work in July 1967 and moved to higher education administration as a financial aid officer. The cultural atmosphere and the trials and tribulations my sons experienced were very different from those of my growing up. Today, those boys have watched their college-age children navigate through a maze of challenges I never knew as a kid. So far, my sons seem to have come through unscathed and are successful in their endeavors. Frankly, I think they were better served not having to wear the mantle of being an eighth-generation pastor.

Great grandfather Squire A. Caris

Great grandfather Enos Peters

Mary Alberta Caris' college yearbook
photograph

Chapter 4

Spiritual Roots

MY SPIRITUAL JOURNEY BEGAN IN THE PARK STREET CONGREGATIONAL CHURCH IN BRIDGEPORT, CONNECTICUT. Park Street Congregational occupied a stately, white clapboard building which stood on Barnum Avenue, a block east of Noble Avenue. The church faced the attractive, tree-shaded Washington Park, a well-kept public amenity covering a full city block. It featured walking paths and park benches, and is still part of the urban landscape. Standing in the park, facing the church across Barnum Avenue, an observer immediately notices the tall steeple rising from the left-hand corner of the building. It still stands watch today, although the church now houses a Spanish-speaking congregation of a different denomination.

Soon after I was born, my name was placed on the Nursery Roll, a fancy poster listing the names of the youngest children in the congregation. It was hung on the wall of the room where infants were cared for while their parents attended Sunday worship. The births of each of my brothers also was recorded on the Nursery Roll: Frank on April 6, 1940; - Alan on May 22, 1942; - Gregory on February 2, 1944. When babies reached three years old, they were moved from the childcare room to participation in a class. They were taught simple stories from the Bible about families and some of the notable figures they would encounter again as they grew older.

Some of the rooms for Sunday School classes were on the lower level of the building. In addition, there was a large open area, known as the undercroft, which provided ample space for social events and gatherings of the congregation. A very functional and sizeable kitchen was adjacent. From the time I could walk, I became well-acquainted with all the rooms and spaces inside Park Street Church, from the social hall and kitchen in the undercroft to the large balcony at the rear of the sanctuary. I still visualize the chancel at Christmas time, with the large Christmas tree and its multicolored lights. During the 1940's a white banner with a red border hung to the right of the chancel. Several blue stars were placed on the banner, each one representing a member of Park Street serving in the military during the Second World War. Over time, several stars changed from blue to gold, representing men who had been killed.

Dad served Park Street from 1934 to the summer of 1947. When my Mother assisted the Sunday School, I was cared for in the nursery school while she played the piano for the children's singing. When I was old enough to sit in church and Mom was busy elsewhere, I usually sat during worship with Mr. and Mrs. Bailey in the pew near the back of the sanctuary. An elevated balcony was located at the rear of the sanctuary. It was used primarily to accommodate occasional overflow attendance. On more than one Sunday as a very young child, I sat with my mother in the balcony so that she could escape with me if I became unruly or disturbed worship in some way.

The balcony held other significance for me. Off to one side were the two offices. One was my father's study and the other the office for the church secretary. Her name was Mrs. McKeever, but I always knew her as "Keever." There were times, in the days before I attended school regularly, when I would be with my Dad and visit the office. "Keever" was always a welcoming person, and while I remember no particular events in the occasional visits to her office as a very young boy, she would become significant at the time of my mother's health crisis when Greg was born.

I have virtually no recollection of participation in Sunday School classes with children of my age during the Bridgeport years. Years later, one youngster from that congregation, Newell Bishop, enrolled in the same class I entered at Yale Divinity School. He sought me out there, and we recalled our time together as youngsters at Park Street church.

Our family left Bridgeport in 1947 and moved to Sandusky, Ohio where Dad was called as the minister of First Congregational Church. There, my participation in the church school, as it had come to be known, was much more regular. I took part in the seventh-grade confirmation class which was the preparation for deciding whether we would become members of the church. This was a very significant decision for me because it involved not only the decision about membership, but also a decision about whether to be baptized. My parents believed in having their children dedicated to God as infants. However, in their view, the decision about both baptism and church membership should be left to each child, usually around the time of his or her thirteenth birthday. This practice is known as believer's baptism. It was an approach to the rite of baptism which had been part of the theology and practice in the Christian Church, or Christian Connection in which my parents had grown up. However, because baptizing as infants was widely accepted among Congregational congregations, my father accommodated parents who wanted their infants baptized.

The confirmation class began in September and usually ran until the end of March. When the class was completed, we each made the decision about whether we wished to formally confess our Christian faith and become members of this particular congregation. The other members of the class had been baptized as infants. And so, on Confirmation Sunday in April, 1950, I was baptized by my father and then confirmed with other members of the class as members of the Christian faith and of First Congregational Church. Both were decisions I took very seriously.

A DECISION FOR THE MINISTRY

Junior high was a time when I was very aware of thinking about a career choice. A vivid recollection about making a career choice has never left me. It is a memory of sitting near the back of the room in my seventh grade English class at Madison Junior High in Sandusky and wondering how I was going to decide what career to choose. How was I going to be able to sustain myself when I had to be dependent on myself to earn a living? In some sense, learning a trade was appealing – perhaps woodworking. I helped Dad back in Bridgeport when he built us a swing and see-saw for our back yard. But I had no idea how I could learn to be a master carpenter. It seemed my Dad was much too involved nights and weekends to be much help in working through the issue. The career issue remained at the back of my mind the rest of the school year without any further meaningful thought. Then, in the summer of 1950, two events became pivotal.

The first was a week at Boy Scout camp. Our troop had signed up to occupy a couple of tents in the woods. Each tent had a wooden platform for a floor. It provided a firm base for four cots. The tent stood about a hundred yards through the woods from the main lodge, which also served as the dining hall. Our gear was stowed on the floor under the cots. This week marked the first time I had spent any length of time away from home. It started on a sunny afternoon, but during the night the rain started to fall. Monday turned into a soggy, miserable day with rain dripping from trees. Trips to the lodge and mess hall for meals became wet and unpleasant slogs along muddy paths through the trees. Obviously, activities were curtailed. The weather didn't improve Tuesday morning.

By this time, I was lonesome, damp and miserable. It felt as if no one in the world cared about me. I could only think about Wednesday evening when my parents were due to show up for the mid-week evening campfire. I was intent on bailing out and going home. When my parents arrived, I told them I wanted to leave. My Dad didn't think that was such a good idea. He was adamant that I stay. And so, I had to tough it out. That night, walking alone through the woods after the campfire, aided only by a flashlight, I felt as if the whole universe was empty except for me and the trees. Not even the stars were visible through the thick canopy of leaves. At least there was a cot waiting at the end of the trail.

I survived through Thursday and Friday, earning a couple of merit badges along the way. I identified enough birds to qualify for birdwatching. The knot-tying badge was the one I truly enjoyed. We did have a shooting range, and I learned to shoot a .22-caliber rifle. However, marksmanship wasn't my forte. I had to be content with the experience.

When I got home on Saturday, I faced a new challenge. I was scheduled to go with two other members of my church youth group to a summer youth camp for junior high young people from churches all over Ohio. Having just had a miserable week at Scout Camp, I wasn't at all interested in being away from home for another week with people I didn't know. Once again, parental influence prevailed. Many arguments were mustered, including the promise that this week would be very different from the last one, especially since we would be housed in cabins with bunk beds, and the program would be very different. The promise was that I would find new friends and return happy that I had participated. There also was the matter of a non-refundable pre-paid camp fee that could not go unused. And so, I went to Camp Chafee, convinced I would be miserable despite my parents' assurances to the contrary.

Of course, the week at the church-sponsored youth conference was an entirely different experience. First, it included boys and girls. Second, it involved a meditation time before breakfast. This was known as "morning watch" and was my introduction to a simple time of guided meditation, using a brief devotional guide at the start of each day. This was a precursor to a spiritual discipline I learned many years later amid a profound emotional crisis.

After breakfast, the program for the morning involved presentations and discussions around a broad theme, usually the study of a particular book of the Bible or a broad topic related to Christian faith. Following lunch, everyone returned to their cabins with their adult counselors and had an hour's rest before the afternoon activities. Various opportunities for crafts and games were available. There always was a softball game, and usually volleyball and badminton as well. Everyone had activities to enjoy. Each evening a big campfire and sing-along rounded out the day.

On the final evening of the summer camp/conference, the closing event was a service of Holy Communion. It was conducted outdoors at a campfire prepared near a small lake. At its conclusion, each of us was provided a candle. The initial candle flame was passed from person to person, until all had been lit. Then we were asked to spread out around the lake and take some time to meditate and pray, or simply to be alone for a time. Although each of us was alone with our own meditations, at the same time, we were a gathered community. I had never experienced a service of worship and Holy Communion in such a setting. It became both emotional and spiritual.

After a period of meditation in the circle of candlelight, I was aware that my attention was turning again toward thoughts about what career I would pursue. The clear sense came to me that God was asking me to prepare for the ministry. This was not an ecstatic experience. It came as a simple conviction that I was being called to the ministry.

It is true that an emotional atmosphere had been created by conducting the service on the last evening of a very meaningful, week-long experience. It is also true that I was set up to be in a very different place after having been through an unhappy week at Scout camp. Even taking these factors into account, I still consider that service, and the sense of calling which arose from it, to be the work of the Holy Spirit calling me to ministry through an unspoken, but nevertheless real and valid Presence. This, to me, was a mystical experience.

A year later, entering high school, I became deeply involved with the Sunday evening church youth group, known as Pilgrim Fellowship. The program addressed many topics. We visited the houses of worship of other faiths to learn about their beliefs and approaches to religious life. We engaged in discussions of major current issues, often bringing in speakers to provide background and facilitate dialogue. We explored our own convictions about these issues and participated in regional gatherings of youth groups from other Congregational churches.

Each summer, I participated in a summer conference for church youth and became increasingly active in the Pilgrim Fellowship. I joined, and eventually led, the Faith Commission, one of three major committees of the state-wide Pilgrim Fellowship. These activities were in addition to a busy schedule of activities in addition to school. These included participating in marching and concert bands, singing in the church choir, continuing with Scouting, and carrying two newspaper routes, the daily afternoon *Register* and the *Cleveland Plain Dealer* before school and on Sunday morning.

In the summer of 1954, after my junior year of high school, I was a delegate to the national meeting of the Pilgrim Fellowship. It was held on the campus of Yale Divinity School (YDS). For a week, I lived in one of the residence houses on the quadrangle and attended worship each day in Marquand Chapel. The discussions and workshops of the conference were held in the same rooms where Dad had studied twenty-two years earlier. It was inspiring to be in the school and the place which had been home to so many great scholars and students for the ministry. Back home in Ohio, I knew and admired several of the ministers who were alumni of YDS, as it was known to many. During the conference, I cherished the day, still five years away, when I might gain admission as a student in the school which already held deep meaning for me.

By the time I reached graduation from high school, my intention to prepare for the ministry was firmly set. I remember my reaction the night I received my high school diploma. "That's one down, two to go," which meant a diploma from college and one from divinity school, a total of seven more years of formal education.

During the years as a student at the College of Wooster (Ohio), I chose not to major in religion. However, in the first year, I was introduced to modern biblical scholarship in two courses: one which surveyed the development of the Old Testament, more commonly referred to as the Hebrew scriptures, and a similar course focused on the New Testament. Later, I had a first course in philosophy. I majored in English and liberal arts courses, got through science with a course in geology and skipped math altogether.

My spiritual journey was nurtured in a variety of ways other than in formal courses. It was a natural extension of my church choir experience at home and an important part of my continuing spiritual life to sing in the choir at Westminster Presbyterian Church on the campus. In addition, as a member of the College's concert choir, I shared in singing some of the greatest choral works, many of which were expressions of profound faith. They included the Brahms *Requiem* and the soaring music of Hayden's

Creation. The performance of Mozart's *Requiem* under Robert Shaw as guest conductor was a profoundly emotional and spiritual experience. When it ended, I was unable to speak and stayed seated for several minutes while experiencing a strong tingling sensation on my face. It was not possible to sing the Latin phrases of the requiem, *dona eis requiem aeternam (grant them eternal rest)*, without being moved to tears, at least I could not.

At Yale Divinity School, I was privileged to sing with the chapel choir. It sang during the morning services in Marquand Chapel. The choir consisted of twenty-four male voices. Today, the student body is virtually balanced between men and women. The distinctive sound of an all-male choir has been replaced by other forms of participation and styles of music which recognize and welcome the diversity of today's students.

The repertoire of the choir in my time at YDS included a broad range of music from the Christian tradition and provided me with an avenue of spirituality quite different from the weekly experience of the choir in a local congregation. The breadth of music was greater, and the quality of singing was better. In those services, I often felt as if I was connected to singers and people of faith from earlier centuries and therefore was part of a continuing heritage of worship through the melodies and sounds heard by countless people of faith. There was a timelessness about the experience which still stirs my heart at the memory of it. Although the forms of musical presentation today may be different from those of an earlier era, they are still timeless, linking worshipers from many times and places.

SOME OBSERVATIONS

The character of my spiritual development as I approached the beginning of formal theological education can be understood from two perspectives. One is my understanding of the character of worship, and the other is the focus of Christian belief, including Christian spirituality, as I had experienced it. I grew up experiencing worship within the Protestant Reformed tradition. This meant that the primary focus of weekly Sunday worship was on hearing the words of Scripture read aloud, and listening to the preacher's homily, or sermon. It usually is intended to be an interpretation of the ways a particular text has meaning for the contemporary hearer. This interpretation may be cast in terms of seeking to illuminate one's personal relationship with God, or in terms of trying to understand how the text illuminates an individual's understanding of a contemporary issue of social justice or one's personal relationships within the human community.

The strong emphasis on interpreting the meaning of Scriptures places importance on seeking to understand the original contexts within which each of the Scriptures were written. Of necessity, such an effort requires an emphasis on learning, and an academic approach to understanding the sources and intent of the situations out of which the many texts of the Bible come. A corollary of this emphasis is that, in the "free church tradition" in which I grew up, each person is free to study, evaluate and adopt theological tenets according to his or her own conscience. Indeed, one of the early definitions of the term "liberal" given to me by my Dad was this notion that a liberal is a person who is free to determine his or her own beliefs and convictions. Thus, in the Congregational churches in which I grew up and which are now part of the United Church of Christ, members are not required to adhere to specific doctrines other than to accept Jesus Christ as Lord and Savior, however the individual may interpret the meaning of that formulation.

The other major elements of worship, as experienced in my formative years, were the prayers and musical expressions of worship in the hymns and anthems which were part of Sunday worship each week. They were the teachers from which I learned to write a wide variety of prayers. Among them were prayers of gratitude and thanksgiving, prayers of confession, and prayers of petition and intercession to God for healing of pain in other persons or restoration of health in one's self. These were the bidding prayers, the prayers of request offered to God. In worship, these prayers might be spoken by the minister or read in unison by the people.

The common characteristic of all these elements was that they represented the individual speaking to God. An entire dimension of prayer, and perhaps the most powerful of them all, was hinted to me by the morning watch experience. Not until I was deeply into the therapeutic process dealing with my childhood trauma, would I discover a vast dimension of the spiritual life which completely changed my sense of connection to the divine. The irony is that I discovered, what was for me, a new pathway to a deeper spirituality through my therapist rather than from the pastors and theological teachers I had known throughout my life.

The next chapters briefly narrate my preparation for ministry, my ordination and first pastorates, before turning to the difficult downhill years and the turning point which led to the beginning of my recovery.

Chapter 5

A Winding Road:

Preparation for Ministry

I WENT TO THE COLLEGE OF WOOSTER WITH EXPECTATIONS OF HAVING AN ENJOYABLE EXPERIENCE, AND FOR THE MOST PART THOSE EXPECTATIONS WERE FULFILLED BEYOND WHAT I COULD HAVE IMAGINED AT THE START. For me, college was to be devoted to academic preparation for the years in divinity school. At the same time, I intended to enjoy more than the academic life. Whatever focus in religious studies I might pursue would be secondary to the goal of exploring the liberal arts in general, an objective built into the required curriculum.

COLD SCOT

One of the joys of my college years came from being a member of the marching Scot band. It was an unusual one. We marched behind a drum major wearing full regalia in the tartan colors of clan McLeod. He was followed by three stout bagpipers and a lone diminutive co-ed who could make the bagpipe skirl as loudly as any of her male counterparts. She was equally resplendent in her McLeod kilt, with proper socks, gleaming shoes and flashing white spats. And every bandsman, or should I say band person, proudly wore the same full-dress uniform with blue tunic and kilt in the McLeod tartan, including all the required accessories. We were the pride of the campus. On Saturday afternoons, when the football team was at home, the fans came from far and near as much to see the band as to watch the game. Formed up in rank order, with bagpipes playing *Scotland the Brave*, the band would begin its march toward the stadium. The crowd in the stadium could hear the distant sounds of the bagpipes and the drummers' steady cadence, at first faint and far away. Then, still out of sight, the sounds grew louder, heralding the oncoming band. Louder and louder it grew, until suddenly the bagpipes and first rows of marchers rose up, as if coming out of the ground as they crested the rise at the west end of the stadium and began the steady march down the slope and onto the field. The drum major signaled the cadence change, and the strains of *When the Saints Go Marching In* echoed across the field. As the crowd broke into applause, we each stepped as smartly as we knew how, eager to look sharp.

After the opening ceremonies and the playing of the national anthem, the band marched to its assigned bleachers opposite the stadium grandstand. On sunny early fall afternoons, this was a delightful place to be. It afforded an unobstructed view of the game. As September faded into the last weeks of October, the afternoon sun grew more distant and less warm. By the time of last game of the season, wearing a kilt could be problematic. Now, I won't reveal what we wore beneath those kilts. But there were occasions when a cold November wind froze one's legs, no matter what permissible item was worn under the folds of a kilt! Thus, it's not surprising that on a cold Saturday afternoon the band marched back to the band room at a much faster tempo than the one it set while arriving.

The concert band also provided both a diversion from study as well as an introduction to many classical pieces and some of the great contemporary works. Just as being part of two campus choirs was a significant element in my spiritual development, these musical experiences were an important and enjoyable part of my college journey.

SILLIMAN UNIVERSITY IN DUMAGUETE CITY, PHILIPPINES

The second memorable experience was the trip to spend my junior year in the Philippines studying at Silliman University on Negros island, four hundred miles south of Manila. The University was founded by Presbyterians in 1901. I lived in the dormitory which housed students in the College of Theology. To students and alumni, the University was known affectionately as Silliman by the Sea. Its history includes surviving occupation by the Japanese military during the Second World War. American faculty members fled to the mountains in the interior of Negros island to hide from the Japanese army at a place called Camp Lookout.

Later, they fled higher into the mountains. Discovered after twenty months in the mountains, they were interned at Santo Thomas prison in Manila until the end of the war. The story is chronicled in a book titled *Escape to the Hills*, written by faculty members James and Ethel Chapman.

During my ten months at Silliman, I was part of an international student group which included Filipinos, Chinese, Thai and Cambodian students as well as four Americans. Eight of us, with a chaperone, travelled from Negros island by overnight island ferry south to Cagayan de Oro on the northern shore of Mindanao. For a week, we visited small communities, schools, church groups, a nursing school and a hospital. The trip ended at Davao on the southern coast. We went by overland truck/bus. The seats were wooden benches and the windows were plain openings. These vehicles transported people and farm animals, mostly chickens. The roof racks were piled with various supplies being delivered to remote communities between larger towns. We saw local culture up close.

Our purpose was to share a message of international understanding, primarily to high school and college students. At one stop, after we had spoken to several hundred students gathered in a school courtyard, we took some questions. Some of them were pointed, demonstrating an awareness of international issues. This particular stop happened a few days after Governor Lester Maddox of Georgia stood in the entrance to a school, brandishing an ax handle and vowing that no African-American student would enter the school. Our questioner wanted to know how we could be travelling and talking about international understanding when there was segregation and intolerance in America. I was chosen to answer. I simply said that we know that America is not perfect, and that we still have a distance to travel to live up to our ideals as they are stated in the Declaration of Independence and the Constitution. At the end of our visit, we were applauded enthusiastically.

I was surprised by the degree to which Filipinos were attentive to events in the United States in the late 1950's. My year there was only a dozen years after the end of World War II and the American presence was still keenly felt. That came home to me one October afternoon as I was walking back from class to my room along the tree-shaded main street of Dumaguete. A young boy, maybe nine or ten years old, came up to me, plucked my trouser leg, and said, "Hey Joe, why doesn't America have Sputnik?" The date was October 4. The news that Russia had launched the first earth satellite wasn't yet a day old when this lad confronted me. I could only mumble that I didn't know why, but I was sure America would have a satellite someday.

One of the most distressing experiences of my year in the Philippines revealed the way in which American practices have impact on other parts of the world. The story began before I left home. Serious delays occurred in obtaining a visa. Two days before my departure, the visa was delivered by registered mail, but it was only for a stay of six months. At this point, it was too late to get the visa corrected to a one-year stay. I would have to work it out once I was in Dumaguete.

The effect of the error was evident soon after I landed in Manila. Philippine immigration asked why I was entering the country. I explained my admission to Silliman for the academic year. "But your visa says six months as a student."

"I know, but it arrived from the consulate in Chicago too late to correct it before I left home."

"Maybe so, but you will have to leave the country by mid-December." By this time, my palms were sweating, and I was struggling to avoid having my voice quiver, never mind the fact that my knees were shaking and my mind was racing, trying to get ahead of what was on the edge of becoming a disaster.

"But, Sir, I'm sure there is a way to revise the visa so that I can complete the year of study," I declared with the best tone of conviction I could muster. In the next moment the negotiation turned to questions about who in Manila was my sponsor.

Eventually my host from the United Church of the Philippines (UCP) was contacted. He had been waiting outside Immigration to greet me and take me to the UCP offices. With a growing sense of relief, I began to feel some degree of hope. With assurances from church officials, I was allowed to remain in the church's hospitality apartment in Manila for the two days it took to complete arrangements. Finally, I was permitted to fly to Dumaguete with one condition. I was to arrange to travel to the consulate in Cebu City on neighboring Cebu Island to have my visa reissued. As it turned out, one other American student had a similar problem with her visa.

And so, a couple of months later, "Nancy" and I found ourselves boarding the early morning ferry for the lengthy trip from Dumaguete to Cebu City on Cebu the island. We arrived about 11:00 a.m., got directions, and headed to the consulate. Soon we were on the second floor of an aging, two-story building. The office was rather stark, with wood floors, and great windows framed in dark, varnished wood. The clerk was behind a service window, protected by an iron grill. Undaunted by her dour demeanor, we presented our documents and asked for new visas which would extend our stay an additional six months. The clerk said processing would take some time. We were told to come back in three hours.

To use the time, Nancy and I explored nearby streets of the city. It was a bustling, noisy urban hub, but much smaller that the bustling metropolis it is today. We found some lunch and passed the time browsing, peering in shop windows and savoring the smells of the open market. The streets were filled with jitneys, the jeep-like taxis seen in every Philippine town of any size. They were modified with brightly painted metal roofs to protect from sun and rain. Nearly every inch of each jitney was lavishly decorated with intricate, multi-colored painted designs in green, yellow, red, and purple and more. Some had colorful fringes hanging from the roof edges. Pictures of the Blessed Virgin, or plastic statues of one saint or another and various family pictures often adorned the dash boards. Only one rule of the road seemed to apply: get to the destination as fast as possible without hitting someone or something, and do so while constantly excoriating every other jitney driver for incompetence.

At the appointed time, we returned to the consulate to discover our visas were not ready. We were told it would be a few more minutes. A half hour went by. No visas. Another half hour passed. Still no visas. Finally, frustrated and realizing that we were beginning to be pressed for time before the ferry to Dumaguete would depart, I went to the clerk's window to ask what was taking so long.

The reply left me speechless. "I don't know why you are so concerned," the clerk said. "You Americans taught us the process." Remembering that the Philippines had been an American protectorate from 1896 until after the Second World War, I curbed my urge to complain further. I politely asked if the visas could be completed soon so that we would not have to miss the ferry back to Dumaguete. In a few more minutes, the visas were produced. I paid the fee, thanked the clerk, and we headed to the ferry pier, grateful that we would no longer have to worry about being deported before the school year was over. Six hours later, darkness had fallen when we arrived on the campus.

My studies at Silliman University included a major research project dealing with the development of Philippine short stories and their place in Philippine literature. This project served as my required Independent Study project for my junior year at Wooster. In addition, some of my courses included the study of Shakespearean tragedies, Philippine anthropology, English literature, and a course on the history of Southeast Asia.

Lost Romance

The third experience which marked my college career was a romance which seemed to be blossoming at the end of my sophomore year. I left for the Philippines having gotten "pinned" to a co-ed who was a junior. Being "pinned" meant I had given her the lapel pin of my men's social group on campus. Wooster did not have fraternities and sororities as such. We were a steady couple not yet engaged, but moving toward a deeper commitment. In the first few months of my year abroad, the letters came fairly regularly. Still, the air-mail correspondence between us took forever because it was carried by propeller-driven airplanes which required several days and fuel stops to traverse nearly ten thousand miles. I began to wonder about the increasingly long delays between letters. Even so, I wasn't prepared for what I learned when I arrived home after eleven months away.

My plan for the return was to leave Southeast Asia April 1958 by merchant ship. However, impatient to get home to my heartthrob, I changed plans and flew back, making visits to Saigon, Angkor Wat in Cambodia, Bangkok, Hong Kong and Tokyo. The return route from Tokyo included a refueling top at Shemya Island in the Aleutians and another at Fairbanks before ending in San Francisco and a two-day visit with relatives. When I finally arrived home, I went to Cleveland to see my sweetheart. To my surprise, in my absence the embers of romance had died. She was now seeing someone else.

I felt some sadness for a few days, but not deep distress about the loss. The long absence had dissolved the connection between us. I did keep for myself the ninety-six pieces of Noritake china that I had ordered shipped from Tokyo. It was to have been a gift for my former flame, but it remained a valued possession in my family and now belongs to one of my sons.

Now, in late May of 1958, my parents were fully involved in preparing to move to Dad's new pastorate in East Cleveland, Ohio. I busied myself reorienting to life in the U.S. I was overwhelmed by the riches in grocery stores and the physical comforts that were far more pleasing than the more spartan, but comfortable, existence in a dormitory on the campus of Silliman University.

In September, I returned to Wooster for my final year of college. The days were filled with researching the required major senior independent study project, a long paper on William Faulkner. To this day, I don't know why I chose such a complex write. The remaining hours of the week were taken up with completing my application to YDS, enjoying the Scot band, the concert choir and church choir as well as a campus job, waiting table at dinner time in the senior women's dorm. I also found time for a major role in G. B. Shaw's *Arms and the Man* and co-writing a pageant skit for the May Day celebration. It was based on Shakespeare's *The Taming of the Shrew*. I rarely dated during that last year.

Shortly after Labor Day in 1959, I began the journey I had been working toward since the summer of 1950 and the youth conference where I first felt the call to prepare for ministry. Now, my parents and I were on the way by car to New Haven, Connecticut and YDS for the start of my seminary studies.

The trip took longer than anticipated. It was after sunset when we crossed from the New York Thruway on to the Massachusetts Turnpike extension. I have never forgotten that night. Not long after darkness fell, a soft yellow-orange glow began to appear in the eastern sky. As the moonrise grew brighter, the silhouetted curves of the Berkshire hills were etched against the night sky. A large luminous disk hung in the darkened eastern sky, bathing the stark landscape in soft moonlight. The nightglow was lighting our way amid the hills and valleys, welcoming us through what might otherwise have been a foreboding and unfriendly journey.

Emerging on the eastern slope of the Berkshires, the road descended into the valley of the Connecticut River. The mist of a light ground fog cast an eerie shimmering along the valley. As far as the eye could see, the ground was covered with a mysterious white carpet, reflecting the now bright moonlight. The strange reflection came from long, wide, gauze-like netting stretched over row upon row of young tobacco plants to protect them from harsh daytime sun, and possible early frost. The scene was unlike any I had ever encountered. I later learned that the soil of the Connecticut river valley produces some of the finest tobacco leaves which are used to provide the last wrapping of prized cigars.

Our destination in New Haven was the home of long-time friends of Mom and Dad, the Rev. Dr. And Mrs. Seldon Humphrey, who were hosting us for overnight. Dr. Humphrey had been on the faculty at Defiance College in Ohio in the 1920s when my folks were students. Even though we arrived after the dinner hour, Mrs. Humphrey insisted that we have dinner. Soon she was filling the dining room table with a wide array of casseroles, vegetables and meat dishes. As one serving dish was depleted, another would take its place. The quantities of food seemed never to diminish. Mrs. Humphrey grew up on a Kansas farm and she still cooked in a style that would feed a hungry crew at harvest time. It seemed her need to assure we had enough food couldn't be satisfied.

The next morning was a gorgeous early fall day, offering a deep blue sky and light breeze. Our arrival at Yale Divinity School was a nostalgic moment for my parents. Dad's Class of 1932 was the first to receive its degrees on the newly constructed campus at the top of the hill on Prospect Street. It was modeled after the quadrangle of the University of Virginia. I had long dreamed of this day, a dream made sharper by a visit to YDS five years earlier for a national youth conference. Now, as we drove in the familiar driveway from Prospect Street, behind the residence houses on the quadrangle, my heartbeat quickened, stirred both by pride and anticipation. Of course, there were many questions. Would I measure up? Would I be able to master the courses? What sort of new friends would I meet? In that moment, I expected this would be home for the next three years. But circumstances change. It would be four years, and a completely new life circumstance before I earned a Bachelor of Divinity degree and began a new career.

My room assignment was 257 in Bacon House, named for Leonard Bacon, one of the great nineteenth century New England clergymen. He was minister of First Church (Congregational) in New Haven. Each of the eight residential houses is named for a prominent member of the clergy. While I was unpacking, my suite-mate arrived. Andrew, who preferred to be known as Randy, was from Winnetka, Illinois. He came from a Presbyterian background, and was a graduate of Stanford University. Personable and gregarious, Randy was a balance to my tendency to introversion. While we were comfortable enough as roommates and enjoyed evening conversations and an occasional game of chess, we spent little time in our suite. Many evenings were spent in the library.

With the transfer of my possessions to my new home completed, and amid the comings and goings of other students getting settled in, Mom and Dad prepared to leave. Assuring them that I had everything I needed, and with a touch of uncertainty, I bid them goodbye. They would spend another day with the Humphreys before returning to Ohio. I turned my attention to preparing for meeting with my adviser to select the courses for the first year.

With the guidance of an advisor, I registered for courses a parish minister would rely upon in his everyday role. The semester included an introduction to the formation of the Bible dealing with the variety of sources for the first five books of the Hebrew Bible, the lives and times of the great prophets, the wisdom literature and the books outside these categories. The second semester dealt with the books of the New Testament: sources of the gospels, the letters of St. Paul, the various minor letters and the complex allegories of Revelation. A two-semester course surveyed church history. Other courses covered preaching, ethics and theological themes in literature. Later courses dealt with methods of pastoral care, elements of the liturgy and history of the sacraments.

Beyond the academic work, many students and faculty members gathered each mid-morning for the daily service in Marquand Chapel. Singing with the chapel choir gave me a sense of connection, not only with great church music selected from across the centuries, but also with a rich source of spiritual nurture. Although barely thirty minutes in length, the highlight of daily chapel was a brief homily or meditation by a faculty member. These meditations frequently provided new insights to the meanings of the text for the day.

Each first-year student intending to prepare for parish ministry had to have a "field work" assignment in a local church on the weekends. This meant we were away from campus all day on Sunday. My roommate, Randy, accepted an assignment at a Presbyterian church in Rahway, New Jersey. To get there he left early every Sunday morning to make the nearly hour-and-a-half drive from New Haven. He often didn't return until near midnight. My assignment turned out to be at the Hamden, Connecticut Congregational Church, a few miles north of the campus on Whitney Avenue. The church faced the local topographic landmark known as the Sleeping Giant, a row of hills providing a silhouette which prompted its identity, which it shared with the state park surrounding it.

By coincidence, the minister was the Rev. Mr. Joseph Peters. He had led Hamden Congregational for long time and was not particularly open to new ways of doing things. My responsibilities included assisting in worship on occasion as well as singing in the choir. The primary role, however, was to develop and guide the youth program, pretty much on my own without other adult leadership, except when the group planned an occasional field trip. This was not particularly challenging because I had grown up in the youth program of Congregational Churches in Ohio. The program and my experiences provided me ample resources and ideas for working with the young people. My year at Hamden Congregational passed uneventfully.

SUMMER, 1960

With the academic year over, I went home to East Cleveland to work a summer job. Through a member of the church, I had a job making small wire brushes in a family-owned machine shop. It specialized in making various sizes of industrial rotary brushes. This was repetitious piece work. I carried a lunch bucket and rode the city bus to and from work each day. I was thankful it was only a summer job.

But if the summer job was boring, after hours were not. At the end of June, the East Cleveland Congregational church held its annual picnic and family outing at nearby Forest Hills park. Of course, the minister's family was there. In addition to food, there were various games to entertain both the younger and older attendees.

Before I realized what was happening, I was being challenged to take part in the egg toss game by an attractive young woman with dark brunette hair and brown eyes. Her name was Karen. Several couples were already lined up facing each other in a parallel line. The women were each given an egg. At the word "go," the holder of the egg tossed it to her partner. Then she took a step back. At the second toss everyone succeeded in passing the egg without breaking. The third toss also was successful. Now the gap in the parallel lines was getting wider. In the fourth toss, several eggs broke, and three or four pairs of hands got very messy!

The double line got shorter, and the gap got wider. On the fifth toss, my partner gently lobbed the egg. I managed to catch it without it breaking. Now the gap was truly wide. I tried my best to toss the egg gently. It arched across the too-wide space, lobbed too high. She caught it over her head. The fragile eggshell collapsed, and the yellow yolk and egg white cascaded into her hair. I was aghast at what I had caused and hastened to try to assist the clean-up. A paper cup and a nearby water fountain provided a means to try to wash out the sticky mess. She took it all in good cheer, eventually finding a towel to begin to dry out her thoroughly soaked head. Although she was being good-natured about the mishap, I expected she would not have much future interest in me. I was wrong. This turned out to be the beginning of a romance. Soon, we were spending a lot of time together, and the summer quickly disappeared.

I returned to Yale in September of 1960. Karen and I wrote to each other regularly. I managed to escape New Haven for Thanksgiving. By Christmastime, we were engaged. I did the proper thing, asking her parents for their permission to marry her. During the break for the holidays, a small engagement party was held in her home in Cleveland Heights. It was attended by our parents and a few select friends. I returned to New Haven in January of 1961 to finish my second year, buoyed by the fact of our engagement. Our plan was to marry eighteen months later, in the summer of 1962, after I finished the second half of my second year and my third year of Seminary.

The field work assignment during my second year at YDS was at the First Congregational Church in Shelton, Connecticut. This assignment was more productive. The Rev. Mr. Ken Taylor was my mentor for the year. On occasion, I sat in on a couple of the congregation's working committees. Ken took personal interest in the development and planning of the youth program, offering guidance and suggestions, but not control. This second-year placement was more in keeping with the intended model for the fieldwork experience. Even so, I had no pastoral care duties and was not asked to preach. More significantly, the program was not providing any feedback about which of my skills were effective and which ones needed to be more fully developed.

The early sixties were a time in theological education in which a new element of pastoral education was gaining acceptance. This was specialized training, usually over the period of a semester, known as clinical pastoral education, or CPE. Such programs focused on the pastor's role in caring for individuals and families who were experiencing crises such as critical illness, major surgery, or bereavement. These programs were aimed at providing insights into the medical, psychological and spiritual dimensions involved in such traumatic experiences. At the time, I was not motivated to search for such a program, and it was not a required element of my preparation. Today, it is a part of the preparation required of many candidates for the ministry. However, I did take a one-semester course in counseling. The text was *Client-Centered Therapy*, by noted psychiatrist Carl Rogers. The course provided me an opportunity to improve my listening skills as well as an introduction to the process and dynamics of psychotherapy.

Doubts About the Ministry

In the course of the spring semester in 1961, I began to wonder if I was headed on the right career path, and I began to consider taking a year to serve in an internship somewhere. The natural place to look for such an opportunity was with the association of churches in the Cleveland area, since the family had moved there in the summer of 1958. I wrote to the executive in charge of the ongoing activities of the Cleveland Union of Congregational Churches, seeking his advice and suggestions. This led to a series of calls and letters which resulted in accepting a two-part internship in Cleveland. It was to begin in early June as soon as final exams were finished.

In all honesty, I have to admit that part of the motivation for taking a year away from my studies was to be near my fiancé. When the decision to do an internship was made, our plan was that we would wait to marry until after I finished my studies in June of 1963. As it turned out, not surprisingly, that plan changed after I was back in Cleveland.

Rob, (upper left) in the baritone horn section,
Wooster Scot Marching Band (1958)

Rob with the International Students Association,
Silliman University, Philippines in 1957 (top row, 3rd from right)

Chapter 6

Internship and Fateful Decisions

T HE YEAR OF INTERNSHIP HAD TWO FOCAL POINTS. The first was essentially a full-time appointment as the research intern with the Regional Church Planning Office in Cleveland, an urban planning organization funded by several denominations. Its purpose was to gather and publish demographic data and information about factors influencing the viability of congregations located in specific communities in the Cleveland metropolitan area. Part of the attraction of this internship was that it was led by a prominent church development planner, the Rev. Lyle E. Schaller. He was a Methodist pastor as well as a trained urban planner. He was also a prolific writer of articles and books about patterns of church growth and the dynamics and factors which influence both church growth and church decline. In order to get a feel for what urban America was about, Lyle had me read Jane Jacobs' seminal book, *The Death and Life of Great American Cities*(1).

The 1960s also were a period in which urban planning involved strong emphasis on the creation of public housing intended to assist low income families. However, the approach often involved the creation of large tracts of low-rise apartment buildings. This was the pattern in Cleveland. In other settings, particularly in New York and Chicago, huge high-rise apartment complexes were erected to accommodate hundreds if not thousands of low-income urban dwellers. These populations tended to be either African-American or of Hispanic and Central American origin. Obviously, these approaches created great challenges, particularly for Protestant denominations which sought to develop new congregations to serve these populations.

At the same time, equally challenging demographic changes were occurring in the so-called first-ring suburbs around core cities such as

Cleveland. During World War II, housing stocks in core cities had become crowded as the influx of labor arrived to work in the war industries. After the Second World War, second-ring suburban communities sprang up. In part, they served the vast numbers of returning military personnel seeking to start families, or to acquire better living conditions. The new communities attracted others who had been living in the first-ring suburbs and now saw the opportunity to escape to newer, better housing. The result was that the populations which had arrived to work in industry during the war now sought better living conditions in the first-ring suburban neighborhoods which slowly were being vacated as their former residents sought to move farther from the city.

All of these changes created challenges for congregations whose members were beginning to leave the communities they had lived in for many years. Many of these established congregations found it difficult to accommodate the religious needs and traditions of the newcomers. Newcomers were establishing their own institutions whose culture and approach were more familiar to the them. Clearly, these changes created difficult challenges not only for established congregations, but also for community leaders, not the least of which was the pernicious effect of racism and the human tendency to resist change.

My introduction to the work with the Regional Church Planning Office was unforgettable. One sunny morning in June 1961, Lyle took me to the southwest side of Akron, Ohio, where he was beginning a study of the churches in the neighborhood. When we arrived, he pulled over to the curb and parked near a major intersection in the chosen inner-city neighborhood. He handed me a note pad and a ballpoint pen and said, "I want you to explore this neighborhood, locate as many churches as you can, store fronts as well as traditional churches, and gather their names and contact information. Also make a note of any community institutions you see. I'll meet you back here in about four hours, and I want you to have made some contacts and arranged appointments with some of the pastors and leaders." Since he had not told me of his plan, I was caught completely off guard.

Clearly, this was a test.

After a few clarifying questions, I was out of the car and beginning my introduction to urban church planning. Lyle intended for me to use shoe leather to get the feel for a community and some of the people first. Understanding maps and census data would come later. My first move was to walk to the gas station in the next block and ask to borrow the telephone book. In those days every station had a phone book which had a section of "Yellow Pages." It included an alphabetic list of businesses and professional people, organized by occupational category, including a section for churches. The directory included maps showing the street names in the study area. After a few minutes I had found the names of several churches, most of them associated with known denominations. Walking through the area, I found several storefront churches, some with a pastor's name and phone number posted on the door or a window. A couple of conversations led me to the neighborhood library and an elementary school. By the time Lyle returned, I had been in several church offices and accumulated the beginnings of a data collection of pastors and community leaders.

Back in the office, I was introduced to census data, census tracts, and the development of census tract maps which displayed population and economic data for each tract. I began to study trends in demographic changes as well as trends in the composition of congregations in a study area, distribution of members by age and sex, as well as changes in total number of members in a congregation over time.

Eventually, after several months of work, a printed report entitled "The Church in Southwest Akron" was distributed for the use of church and community leaders. This was one of several studies prepared in the course of my internship, but it was the only one which began with my being summarily left on a street corner to find my way!

The project which occupied the largest portion of my time focused on the City of East Cleveland and its churches. In addition to gathering comparative population and economic data for census tracts in the city, a survey of church members was developed to gather statistics about number of years of membership, composition of the membership by age and gender, numbers of children enrolled in youth programs, etc. Some of these statistics were available over a period of years so that trends could be discerned. The final document was presented to the churches which participated in the study.

GLENVILLE CONGREGATIONAL UNITED CHURCH OF CHRIST

The second part of the internship year was devoted to serving as the "stated supply minister" for an older Congregational Church located on a busy street corner surrounded by retail business in the Glenville neighborhood on the east side of Cleveland. The "stated supply" phrase describes a minister assigned as the temporary pastor while the congregation is determining its future, which usually means conducting the search for the next full-time minister. Today the term "interim pastor" or "transitional pastor" usually is used in these situations. The Glenville neighborhood was, in fact, a first-ring suburban community in transition from a predominantly white population to an increasingly African-American community. In many ways, the future of Glenville Congregational Church was in doubt. The history of its decline could be plotted easily. It was an illustration of the effect of long-time residents opting to move to farther out suburbs and their places being taken by people leaving the core city.

Ultimately, the decision was made that the church would close and the building be sold with the proceeds being used by the denomination to support church growth elsewhere in the Cleveland region. A year after the sale of the building to an African-American congregation, it was once again a bustling house of worship with an active program in the community.

In the meantime, the few remaining members, less than fifty, needed to be served by a pastor. Thus, I was granted a ministerial license to serve as Glenville's pastor. I conducted worship and the sacraments, made some pastoral visits, and helped provide guidance to the congregation as it worked with the denomination to make decisions about its future. In significant ways, my introduction to parish ministry was negative. Not long after I started my year, the real situation became clear: this congregation could not survive. In the first place, it could not generate sufficient financial resources to provide even part-time pastoral care and also meet the cost of upkeep and utilities for a sizeable old building. Further, I discovered that the neighborhood organization dedicated to resisting the influx of non-white families was holding its monthly meetings at the church. The image presented to the community was negative. Denominational leaders and I began the process of working with the congregation to prepare for closing and transferring the property to the denomination. This was, in effect, a significant death of a congregation that had served the early days of its neighborhood on the eastern edges of the city limits of Cleveland. Now, in the early 1960s, it had lived into maturity and aged past its viability while the community matured and then watched much of its population be replaced with newcomers.

During my time with the congregation, I conducted my first funeral. It was for an elderly, long-time member of the church. I had attended funerals conducted by my father and had many of the scripture passages and poetry selections he used. His model for a service included selections from these materials and prayers, some of which were tailored to reflect the life of the deceased person. The service usually included a brief summation of the person's life offered by the minister. In the few services I had experienced, this narrative was not an occasion to dwell on the nature of the afterlife or how one should prepare for it. I did experience, in some funerals I attended, eulogies in which the minister included a somewhat morbid exhortation to prepare for judgment day or endure the negative consequence of failing to do so.

My own early experiences with death and the emotions related to it were constrained and largely held close. The one experience of spontaneous tears I remember came during the winter of my second year in seminary when I received the call from my father telling me that my grandfather, with whom I was always very close, had died. I went for a long walk that evening, trying to absorb a kind of pain I had not ever felt before. And yet, at his funeral, my emotions were very much in check. Without other resources, my father's model was the one I followed when I presided over the first funeral of my career during the year of internship.

Many years later I learned more positive ways in which such services could be planned as a service of worship as well as a memorial celebration of the deceased person's life. In such services, the pastor's remembrance may be based on a passage of scripture which provides a metaphor for the life and achievements of the one who has died. Frequently, family members and others are invited to share vignettes and remembrances that are warm and illustrative of the legacy of the one who died. This newer approach to memorial services allows family and mourners to acknowledge both the reality of grieving and the ongoing positive legacies of the deceased person, even when tragedy has occurred.

This was not the atmosphere of the first funeral service conducted during my months at Glenville Congregational Church. Each reading of scripture, intended to reassure the widow, only elevated her distress. While the period of spoken prayers seemed to provide some solace, she remained largely inconsolable. But the most difficult moments were still to come. She and her husband had opted for cremation of his remains. I anticipated that I would accompany the funeral director in his car as he led the hearse to the cemetery. Once there, after the casket placed on a dolly taken to the doorway of the crematory, I would offer a prayer and then the Words of Commendation of the deceased into the everlasting care of God, to be followed by a final benediction. The funeral director would take care of any instructions to the crematory staff and we would leave.

The widow had other plans. She insisted that she and a few family members ride to the cemetery in a car which would follow the funeral director and the hearse to the cemetery. I was to ride in the hearse with the funeral director. She declared she must accompany the casket to its final end. Thus, on a very rainy, gray and overcast day, the little cortege drove to the cemetery. When we arrived, the funeral director and an assistant placed the casket on a dolly and wheeled it into the crematorium. It was a surreal sight with a casket on its dolly, a funeral director, myself in a simple black robe and a grieving widow standing in this eerie and unnerving place. Somehow, I managed to read the prayers for Commendation and conclude the Benediction. As the casket was being placed in the crematory, the funeral director was able to convince the widow that the wishes of her husband were being followed. He persuaded her to leave the building. She did. I, too, stepped outside. After spending a few moments with the widow, I escaped to the hearse and the chance to regain some sense of the normal.

While the first funeral I ever conducted was difficult and out of the ordinary, other elements of the experience with the Glenville Congregational UCC were enjoyable and instructive. They helped me begin to feel the rhythms of the week-in-and-week-out flow of a congregation's life. This was different from what I knew growing up in a minister's home. Now I was responsible for planning worship in relation to both the ordinary and the celebratory events in the church year. Pastoral care, even in a small congregation, required setting aside specific times for visits to individuals as well as being able to respond to the unanticipated need from a person facing surgery or other crisis. What was missing from this assignment, however, was the challenge of coordinating the month-to-month program activities of various groups.

The Glenville church had shrunk to the point where only one governing body needed to care for administrative affairs. Groups such as Deacons, or a spiritual care committee or mission program committee had long since ceased to exist. There were no separate men's or women's fellowship groups, nor was there a Christian Education program providing weekly church school classes because there were no longer any young families involved. Without such groups present and operating, the internship experience offered no real opportunity to learn the ins and outs of maintaining a complex church program. Thus, the internship experience did not equip me with an understanding of the effective methods for facilitating the decision-making work of volunteers in the organizations which comprise the program structure of a congregation. This would prove costly in subsequent years after ordination.

In spite of the limited time I had with them, the members of the Glenville Congregational Church were able to arrange a very meaningful final Service of Worship and Thanksgiving in honor of the church's many years of ministry to the community. It was held early in 1961. Leaders of the Congregational Union of Cleveland were in attendance, offering words of appreciation for the congregation's history. They were sincere in their gratitude for the decision to transfer the church property to the denomination. The proceeds from the sale of the building were used to support church growth in other locales. I did not have any other pastoral assignments during the internship.

Change in Plans

In the early summer of 1961, not all of my focus was on the tasks of my internship. Now that we were living with our respective families, my fiancé and I were together most evenings and a portion each weekend. Earlier in the spring before I left New Haven, it became increasingly clear that we did not want to wait a year and a half to marry. After I was home, we had negotiated an agreement to celebrate the wedding on December 30. As it turned out, other changes were in the offing as well. Late in the summer, Dad accepted an appointment to become a member of the senior staff at our church's national offices in New York City. His new work was to begin in early January. One of his last services was to conduct our wedding just before leaving the church in East Cleveland.

This change also affected Mom and my brothers. Frank was in his junior year in college. Alan was a freshman, and Gregory still had to complete his senior year of high school. Although Mom could stay in the church's parsonage for a period of time before a new pastor was called, plans would have to be made for a move to New York. I would be involved in our search for an apartment and making it ready to become our home after the wedding. As the summer merged into fall, my days became increasingly busy.

Mentoring

As part of the internship, I was assigned a mentor with whom I could meet periodically. The minister of the nearby Collinwood Congregational Church was my guide. Our relationship was largely unstructured. We met occasionally for lunch, sometimes followed by further conversation in his office. We ranged over topics related to issues of growth and change confronting urban churches, including racial conflict, urban decay in the core city, and new patterns of ecumenical cooperation seeking to address issues of poverty, tenants' rights and effective advocacy in the halls of local government. The Collinwood church was a much larger congregation and had not yet faced the kind of decline which had overtaken Glenville.

These luncheon conversations also became the occasion for introducing me to social drinking. I had not yet participated in many occasions where cocktails were served, other than to attend an occasional wedding reception. Our usual pattern was to meet for lunch. My mentor frequently ordered a cocktail. At age twenty-four I was a teetotaler. Early in the relationship I expressed interest in being able to socialize comfortably where alcohol was being served. The previous summer my family had attended a backyard picnic at the home of friends. Some folks were having drinks, including the young lady I had started to date. Somewhat surprised and frankly, taken aback, I continued to avoid alcohol. Now, in the summer of my internship, a year later, I was encountering more social situations where drinks were available. Refusing offers of drinks gave me feelings of not fitting in with others. At first, when my mentor ordered a cocktail at lunch, I would order coffee or nothing. But in time, he suggested a highball of bourbon and water. Soon, I was having a drink at the start of our luncheons. In time, I grew to like Manhattans which were comprised of sweet vermouth and whiskey. My taste for alcohol had expanded.

Marriage and Transitions

By Christmas, the midpoint of the internship had arrived. I celebrated Christmas with my Mom and Dad and brothers. In addition, my folks were busy with preparations for our wedding. It took place on December 30, 1961 at East Cleveland Congregational Church. Dad performed the ceremony and the modest reception was held in the social hall of the church. Of course, the church was still decorated for Christmas. My bride's mother made the wedding cake. The only hitch in the festivities was the snow which began to fall while the wedding and reception were underway. By the time we were ready to leave, several inches of snow were on the ground. I had arranged an overnight in a motel about thirty miles away. Weary but happy, we arrived safely.

The next day we drove to Toronto for a brief honeymoon at a resort overlooking Lake Ontario. The second day, we came down with a bug that left us too ill to do anything. By the time we recovered, our brief stay was over. We returned home, vowing we would find another way to have a more enjoyable celebration. We were wonderfully surprised to find that while we were away, my bride's father and the father of her maid-of-honor had stocked the refrigerator and pantry with enough foodstuffs to support us for a month!

Our walk-up apartment was not far from my parents' home. It was in a classic apartment building with beautiful dark woodwork trim on windows and doors. We lived there for eight months until August, when we packed for our move to New Haven and my final year in seminary.

My year of internship brought major changes to my life. I had experienced a degree of parish work, although it involved guiding the final demise of the congregation I served. I discovered a whole new world involving urban planning, and enjoyed it so much I toyed with studying city planning at the University of North Carolina. I learned to be comfortable with social drinking, and I was returning to New Haven and an apartment for married students instead of the single-sex residential houses on Sterling Quadrangle.

One other significant decision had been made. During the summer, I was invited to take part in a special program at the Divinity School for the coming year. It was to be a hands-on seminar with a group of eight students who would study under the guidance of an experienced pastor and be involved in specific parish activities. I had to make the decision while still in

Cleveland and several weeks before the new semester began. I chose not to be part of the group, thinking I wanted to pursue other activities. Whatever I thought I wanted to do instead is long forgotten. It is a decision I regretted after my later experiences in two very different congregations.

FACING NEW DOUBTS

Still enjoying the role of newlyweds, we returned in mid-August to New Haven by way of Newport, Rhode Island and a visit with friends. It was festive time to be in Newport. The town was hosting the America's Cup yachting competition with an Australian yacht. Being near the boat docks and watching the crews prepare for the races inevitably drew us into the air of excitement on the waterfront. The weather hinted at the coming autumn. The morning air was clear and cool. A light breeze brushed the water just enough to make the sunlight sparkle off the dancing ripples in the bay. It was hard to say goodbye to our friends and leave behind those two relaxing and pleasant days.

I turned my attention to the final year in seminary. For the most part, the course load was manageable. However, as September merged into October, I found myself feeling an increasing uncertainty about whether I was really on the right path. Part of the difficulty probably was an understandable unease which might be expected as a person approached the time when the academic life would shift to the reality of a day-to-day job serving a congregation. I was finding it difficult to focus on academic work, and it seemed a deeper uncertainty was stirring about whether I really wanted to enter the ministry. Some of the uncertainty was caused by my exposure to urban church sociology and city planning in the course of my internship. That experience motivated me take a course at the Yale Graduate School on the rise of European cities and the influence of geography in their development. I was toying with trying to enroll in the city planning program at University of North Carolina.

Near the end of October, I decided to go to New York to seek my Dad's counsel. One morning, I boarded the train to the city and met my Dad for lunch near his office in lower Manhattan. There was an Episcopal church around the corner from his building. It served an inexpensive soup and sandwich lunch. It was an ideal spot for a conversation away from the din of the city. I shared with Dad my doubts and struggles about becoming a parish minister. We talked about what seemed to be causing my distress. "Would I really find satisfaction in parish work?" "Could I manage the administrative side?" We came to no clear answers to these and other questions. The decision remained unresolved. Finally, he said to me that he couldn't tell me what to do. He did say he believed that if I gave up finishing the divinity degree, a day would come when I would regret having done so. He felt that if I could finish the work, even if I chose not to be ordained right away, I would have the degree in the event I decided, later on, to be ordained.

I boarded an afternoon train back to New Haven. As I watched the coastal towns pass by the train windows, I remembered hearing earlier stories of my parents living through the financial challenges of Dad's last year in seminary in 1932. They were down to their very last nickel and thought they would have to leave school. Dad went to the dean, who urged him to stay. A way would be found. A few days later, Dad was awarded a prize in preaching, the grand sum of $100, which enabled him to stay and graduate. I resolved to stay on and finish what I had started.

The train arrived in time for me to attend a dinner sponsored by the New Haven Council of Churches. As it turned out, this was the evening, October 22, 1962, when President Kennedy delivered, at 7:00 p.m., his address announcing the Cuban Missile Crisis and the use of the American navy to quarantine the island and prevent cargoes of offensive weapons from reaching Cuba. The broadcast was aired in the banquet hall to an absolutely silent audience. While at lunch with Dad, we heard that the President was to speak in the evening. However, I did not pick up on the gravity of the topic until I was at the banquet. The memory of that day has never left me.

As the spring wore on, my decision about the future was determined in part by necessity and in part by the thought that if I did not like parish work, I could find an alternative at some point in the future. When a representative of the Ohio Conference of the United Church of Christ came to YDS to interview potential candidates for positions in the churches of the Conference, I met with him. My name and ministerial profile were submitted to the Hambden Congregational Church (United Church of Christ). The ministerial profile is a lengthy document completed by candidates for positions in the churches. If I were to be selected, I knew I would have a way to support my family.

Eventually, I received a letter from the chair of Hambden church's pastoral search committee asking about my interest in the church. Other correspondence followed and I interviewed in person later in the spring. Eventually, I accepted the church call to become its pastor and teacher.

Before turning to the conclusion of my time at Yale Divinity School, it is worth sharing one of the special experiences of those years. I cherish memories of the annual Christmas celebration held each year in the Common Room, a large comfortable room for sitting, reading and conversations with friends. It also was the place where students gathered before the doors to the refectory opened at meal times. At other times, the Common Room was the gathering place for coffee hour after morning chapel, or for other events for the wider community.

Each year in the Christmas season, the community came together to hear Professor Roland Bainton deliver from memory portions of Martin Luther's Christmas sermons. The professor was an eminent scholar on the works of Martin Luther and was widely known as an expert in church history. He vividly portrayed the story of the birth of Jesus in Luther's words, highlighting Luther's particular emphasis on the common folk who were the participants in this very human story. Luther had a distinctive way of focusing on the common folk whom God chose for God's gift to humankind. Professor Bainton could deliver Luther's insights in a way which dramatized the contrast between the hustle and bustle of Bethlehem, crowded as it was with travelers arriving to answer the required census, and the unassuming arrival of God's gift to the world.

I was pleased that my wife, Karen, was with me for my last year at YDS and heard this moving presentation of Luther's imagery of the common folk and their daily struggles in this timeless story. I still have on my shelf a copy of Bainton's small, paper-bound book entitled The Martin Luther Christmas Book. (2) It is illustrated with reproductions of Albrecht Durer's woodcuts of the various elements of the Christmas story. On occasion, I have shared excerpts of Luther's words with gatherings at Christmas. My listeners always express appreciation for Luther's perspectives on the story.

On to Graduation

My resolve to complete my studies turned out to be more difficult than I anticipated. The added difficulty was of my own making. In the last semester I needed one course to fulfill the graduation requirements. I opted for a course my father had taken thirty years earlier. I did not anticipate its degree of difficulty. The professor, Dr. Calhoun, had taught the history of Christian doctrine thirty years earlier when my father had taken it. I thought it would be a fun thing to do. Dad and I would have an experience in common.

To complete the course, students were required either to take a final exam, or to write a fifty-page paper on a topic of their choosing. I chose the paper because I realized I did not have enough background to truly understand some of the material in a course designed for Ph.D. students in theology. My topic was on an aspect of St. Augustine's theology. I was in over my head! It's likely a graduate student graded my paper. He gave me a "D," the lowest grade I ever earned. Basically, I got credit for taking the course, and thus was able to graduate. It might have helped if I had taken a semester or two of Greek, since most of the lecture on the Nicene Creed was in Greek. Several other theological complexities were equally opaque. Clearly, there are some subjects in which I am not a scholar.

The fact that I just got by in my last course did not dampen my excitement about finishing seminary. Graduation day was glorious, even though Mom and Dad were attending my brother Frank's graduation from the College of Wooster. A new future was ahead, and I was relieved to know that a new ministry and position were waiting. They would enable me to support my wife and unborn son. My father's assurance that I would not regret having finished seminary was true. To this day, I cherish my time at Yale Divinity School and have actively supported it for more than half a century.

NOTES

1. Jacobs, Jane, *Death and Life of Great American Cities*, (New York, Random House, 1962).

2. Bainton, Roland, *The Martin Luther Christmas Book*, (Philadelphia, Muhlenberg Press, 1948), 75 pages.

Chapter 7

Ordination and Two Congregations

P REPARATION FOR ORDINATION IS A LENGTHY PROCESS. In the free church tradition of the Congregational Christian churches and their successor, the United Church of Christ, candidates for ordination are examined by the Committee on the Ministry, a group made up of clergy and lay representatives from the association of congregations in a defined geographic area. The candidate first is asked to present evidence of appropriate qualifications for ordination. These include a four-year Bachelor of Arts degree and a three-year Bachelor of Divinity degree now defined by many schools, of which Yale is one, as a Master of Divinity. In addition, I was required to be under the guidance of a minister during a period of discernment about my desire to pursue ministry as a career. This period is designed to sharpen and strengthen the candidate's clarity about the sense of calling to the Christian ministry.

Discernment with my mentor began when I was a senior in high school and continued through the college years. After completing theological training, I was interviewed by the Committee on the Ministry, which was comprised of clergy and lay members of the Plymouth Rock Association of churches in which I was to be ordained. With the committee's approval, the next step was to prepare an ordination paper laying out my theological views, my steps of preparation, and my understanding of the role and the work of a pastor. The final step was to present the paper and be questioned about it by an Ecclesiastical Council, a gathering of clergy and lay representatives of the area churches of my denomination.

My ordination service was to take place in the Hambden (Ohio) Congregational Church, United Church of Christ on Saturday, August 30, 1963 at 8:00 p.m. This was the church I had been called to serve. Hambden was a small crossroads town in eastern Geauga County, thirty-five miles east of Cleveland. My strong preference had been to begin my ministry in Ohio. This proved to be a limitation. In the spring of 1963, my final semester of seminary, it was time to seek my first call to a congregation. I wanted to serve as the pastor in a congregation rather than as a member of a pastoral staff. As it turned out the one solo position open in northern Ohio was in a small country church east of Cleveland. I had expressed interest only in Ohio, preferring to locate near my wife's parents since my parents were located in New York City.

In addition to the tension of seeking a first pastorate, my wife and I were expecting our first child in September. I was feeling the pressure to find employment. After two trips to Ohio for interviews, the congregation at Hambden voted in May to call me as their pastor. The vote was not unanimous. With no other opportunities on the horizon, I accepted the call. In hindsight, the lack of unanimity should have alerted me to discord and caused me to turn down the offer. Anxious to secure a job, I minimized the red flag and accepted the call.

Having finished at YDS, we made plans for moving back to Ohio. Our few possessions consisting of household goods, books and a few pieces of furniture were loaded into a rented trailer. We towed it behind our little Volkswagen "bug." The house that was to be our home was ready for us in July. We moved in, got settled and I began work. Together with members of the church, we put the final touches on arrangements for the service of ordination and the reception to follow.

THE SERVICE

The Saturday of the ordination service was hot and muggy, and by evening the air was still close and oppressive. Even so, the small country church was filled to capacity for an ecclesiastical event which had not happened since the founding of the congregation more than a hundred years earlier. In addition to ordination, the service included the rite of installation of the new minister as pastor and teacher. I would be the first pastor to serve the church full-time. This would be a new experience for both the congregation and me.

The ordination service was especially significant for me because my father was a participant. I invited the Rev. Dr. Ben M. Herbster, President and General Minister of the United Church of Christ, to deliver the ordination sermon. I know he accepted because Dad was a member of Dr. Herbster's staff. I was deeply honored, and so was Dad, to have him as the preacher for the service. Following the sermon, Dad offered the Prayer of Ordination. At the end of the service, he participated in helping me don a minister's robe as a symbol of the conclusion to the ordination. The presentation of the Certificate of Ordination and a stole followed by the Benediction.

Because there are many elements in an ordination and installation, several of the people who had nurtured and guided me during my formative years were participants. I had hoped one of them would be the Rev. Eleanor Galusha who, in the 1950s, was one of the minority of women pastors in our denomination and the only one in the local area association of churches. She was my mentor and counselor in high school and college while I held the status of "in care" of the local association of churches. She guided me through the process of discernment about my call. Unfortunately, she had moved from Ohio and was not able to be present.

The composition of the pool of candidates for ordination as well as the membership of the clergy has changed dramatically in the fifty-five years since my ordination. In hindsight, I am aware that every participant in that service was male. There were no women pastors, no women readers of Scripture, and no women chairs of any of the committees with which I worked in the process of the interviews. Today, any ordination conducted in the United Church of Christ most likely would reflect a balance of both men and women as leaders and participants. Many ordination services in the United Church of Christ also include representatives from African-American, LGBTQ, and other minority communities. The denomination's commitment to diversity and "extravagant welcome" is genuine. While an increasing number of churches make purposeful efforts to become significantly more diverse, the great majority of congregations remain predominately white. As a small rural congregation, the membership of the Hambden church did not include non-white members.

Feelings and Emotions

The feelings and emotions that come in the ordination experience are like no others. Ordination happens once and is intensely personal. I was aware that my life would be forever changed, but only later would I discover many of the implications of that reality. Writing now, more than five decades after the event, many emotions remain crystal clear. I felt deep appreciation for so many people who had been mentors and guides along the journey to this moment. I knew that I was entering into a total commitment to serve the Christian faith I had professed at age thirteen at First Congregational Church in Sandusky.

At the front of the church, three steps led to a raised platform area called the chancel. It was the location for the pulpit on the left, the Communion Table in the center and to the rear, and the seating for the choir on the right. Following the sermon, I was invited to kneel on the first step leading to the chancel platform for the Prayer of Ordination and the Laying on of Hands. As I knelt there, the gathered ministers from the churches of the Plymouth Rock Association, led by my father, each laid a hand on my head or shoulders as my father delivered the prayer.

Considering the number of participants in the service, as well as the many ministers from area churches in attendance, there must have been more than a dozen pairs of hands on my head and shoulders. At first, I did not notice the cumulative weight. Gradually, the pressure from the weight of the hands, and the closeness of the air around me were increased. The long ministerial robes surrounding my kneeling figure blocked out any fresh air that might have been stirring that muggy evening. The backs of my thighs began to quiver and the hamstrings started to tense. The thought came that I might not be able to last to the end, or be able to stand if I did. My mind was not on my father's prayer except to wonder when it would end! Actually, it probably took no more than three minutes. As I heard the concluding "Amen," I was relieved to feel a hand under each arm gently helping me to stand.

Immediately following the ordination, representatives of the association of churches as well a representative of the congregation offered words of congratulations. In these moments, as events were happening, almost in rapid-fire succession, a growing realization came to me. Whatever the future might bring, my life was changed and would be forever colored and shaped by the fact that I had made this public commitment to serve God in this visible way. I could not predict where the path I had entered would lead. In the coming years, my hopes for where the promises I made might lead would be dramatically reshaped.

HAMBDEN CONGREGATIONAL CHURCH

The members of the Hambden church were looking forward to having their first full-time pastor. The township was a rural farming community and had not seen any meaningful expansion until after World War II. A few small pockets of new housing had been built in the area, and there was hope that real growth would come to the eastern part of Geauga County as it had to the area west of Chardon, the county seat.

In Hambden, the relatively small white clapboard church with its steeple faced U.S. Route 6, known as the Grand Army of the Republic Highway. It was east of an intersection with state highway 58. The parsonage, a white clapboard building with green shutters, stood west of the church on the northeast corner of the intersection facing the state highway which ran north and south. West of the house, across the state highway, was a small gas station and convenience store.

The church had refurbished the parsonage, a building rumored to have served at one time as a boarding house. Now it had the feeling of newness, with freshly painted walls and woodwork and new vinyl tile flooring throughout. To the north of the house, enterprising members of the congregation had plowed up and planted a substantial garden space. Apparently, I said something in my interviews about hoping to have a garden one day.

We arrived in midsummer and were astonished to find an immense garden already well-established. It appeared to be at least twenty-five feet wide and seventy-five feet long. There were rows of corn, lettuce, tomatoes, beans, peas, radishes and more. Already some plants were yielding a harvest. The corn was getting close to ready for picking. Among the sea of flourishing plants, a healthy crop of weeds was in need of serious intervention. If we wanted the joy of the harvest and a garden that was not overwhelmed by unwanted invaders, we would have to do some serious weeding work.

In the midst of all this, our first child was due to arrive in little more than a month. Weeding would fall to me alone. I chose a nice sunny Sunday afternoon to tackle the job. I made slow headway, and much remained. Later in the week, I happened to be outside when the elderly lady who lived across the highway beckoned to me to come over. She wanted to tell me something. She had been chatting with a member of the congregation who was complaining about the new young minister.

"Oh?" I responded, "What was the problem?"

Well," came the reply, "Mrs. So-and-so thought it was not right that the minister was working in the garden on Sunday."

"Well, what did you say?"

"I told her that it seemed to me the better the day, the better the deed!" After a pause she concluded: "I just thought you'd like to know."

And so, I learned the first lesson of living in a small town. My father used to call this sort of conversation the "bush telegraph." It was in fine working order in Hambden.

The initial months of getting to know one another were going well. The fall and winter were a time for pastor and people to discover each other's expectations. I needed to make adjustments. These included being willing to accommodate the fact the teachers in the Sunday school program had chosen to use non-denominational teaching materials. The teachers found them easier to use than denominational resources. Among some leaders there was an expectation that I would arrange to visit church families in their homes. Some families were open to the idea, others less so. I did make it a point to visit individuals who were hospitalized, and I took my turn serving as the chaplain of the week at the local hospital. In a small congregation, there was not a heavy load of grief counseling or pastoral care needed by individuals facing serious crises.

Additional stresses were created as America was confronted by the expanding Civil Rights Movement. The historic March on Washington when The Rev. Dr. Martin Luther King, Jr. gave his famous *I Have a Dream* speech happened on the Wednesday before I was ordained. President John F. Kennedy was assassinated two months later. It was a difficult time in which to try to interpret current events in the light of the Christian concern for social justice and peacemaking.

These issues became more difficult in the spring of 1964 when the civil rights crisis became critical in Cleveland amid efforts to resolve issues related to de-facto segregation in the Cleveland public schools. One of the tragic events in the city occurred when a young Presbyterian minister who had graduated from YDS the year before me was killed accidently during a protest demonstration at a school construction site. In the summer of 1964, the spouse of the choir director at the Hambden church, a science teacher in the local high school, asked me to support his application to be a teacher in the Mississippi Freedom Schools Project. I did so. At the same time, I was hearing from church members who felt that the civil rights crisis was not an appropriate topic for my sermons. A minority of folks felt the issue was in the category of politics and not to be discussed in church. In spite of these differences, we maintained the regular program and activities through the fall, the holiday season and through 1964.

There were expectations that calling a new minister would soon result in a noticeable growth in membership and financial resources. There were few signs of such growth. The community was not seeing any noticeable increase in new residents. Moreover, my own inexperience and tendency to want new ways of organizing and developing programs met with reluctance and doubt.

In early 1965, it was becoming increasingly difficult for us to find common ground. I asked the staff person in our area denominational office responsible for ministerial placement to assist me in finding a new call. Meanwhile, our second son was born on the first of March. Now three human beings were dependent on me. After several interviews, and a trial sermon in a neutral pulpit, I received and accepted a call to become the minster of the North Ridgeville Congregational Church, west of Cleveland, not far from Elyria, Ohio. This was a congregation of more than three hundred and fifty members in a well-established town, consisting of many multi-generational families as well as new residents employed in nearby offices and industrial firms. We moved to our new home in April.

NORTH RIDGEVILLE CONGREGATIONAL CHURCH

I arrived in North Ridgeville when the congregation was in the final months of a renovation of its sanctuary and exterior. The chancel was redesigned so that a pulpit stood at one side of the platform and a lectern on the other. Fresh paint on the inside, and a sandblast cleaning of the yellow brick exterior along with repainting the outside of the window frames in an olive green created the feeling that the church was entering a new chapter in its history.

This was a congregation of more than three hundred members. Many were working class people employed in nearby manufacturing plants. Others were professionals including teachers, lawyers and health care workers as well as small business owners. Part of the new challenge was to develop a good working relationship with the paid staff. The choir director and organist, church secretary and custodian all were part-time paid positions. Many positions were filled by volunteers, including the elected officers of the church council and the leaders of boards and committees. It was a strong and effective group.

As happened in Hambden, this also turned out to be a two-year pastorate. A youthful mistake in judgement caused some individuals to be concerned that I was not fully focused on my duties. I auditioned and was chosen for a role in the local Little Theatre production of G.B. Shaw's play *Arms and the Man*, the same role I had played in college. Not being well-attuned to the fact that some members would think I was not giving enough time to my duties, I made the mistake of not getting approval from the church council before undertaking the role. This, in spite of the fact that rehearsals and production took place in the evening and on my own time. Of course, a promotion photo of the leading lady and me appeared in the local paper, along with a review of the show. That set off some very active discussion which took a while to calm.

The more challenging issues again were related to controversies in trying to deal both with the civil rights issues and now, more prominently, the Vietnam War. The teenagers were very much concerned about the issue of the selective service and the military draft. This was the period when some individuals were fleeing to Canada to avoid military service and others were burning draft cards. Somehow, one parent of a teenager developed the notion that I was counseling high school students to resist the draft. What few discussions we did have were about the meaning of protest, the concept of conscientious objection and what it meant to struggle with issues of conscience. The young people discussed what it meant to face and accept the consequences of various forms of protest. This was not a case of promoting a specific way to respond once a young person reached the age for registering with a military draft board.

LEAVING THE MINISTRY

Once again, divisions of opinion about my leadership had arisen, and the potential for a serious split in the congregation was developing. Earlier in the spring, a denominational leader called a meeting to allow members of the congregation to express both positive and negative concerns. This turned out to be a highly contentious meeting which did not result in a proposal for resolving the issues. I realized that the actual effect of the meeting was to widen the rift. There were those who urged me to allow a vote about my future in North Ridgeville, believing I could win. I realized such a move would further damage the congregation. I announced my intention to resign later in the spring of 1971.

After several weeks spent in a job search, I accepted an appointment as Assistant Director of Student Financial Aid at Case Western Reserve University in Cleveland. In June of 1967, we moved to Cleveland Heights. We bought our first home with a loan of funds for a down payment from my wife's parents. It was paid back in full over the next four years. This was our first step in building equity in a home of our own.

A significant follow-up to the story of the teenagers' discussion about civil protest occurred several months after I left North Ridgeville. The parent who accused me of counseling the teens to adopt a particular response to the Vietnam War came to my home in Cleveland Heights to apologize for having made the accusation. I was completely surprised and had great respect for his having done so.

This career change was the first of a series of positions in the non-profit world with non-profit educational and human service organizations. Although I enjoyed these jobs, my personal life was moving into what I have termed the downhill years. I would not again serve as a full-time local pastor. Instead, my spiritual life was limited to attending Sunday worship and volunteer roles in church-related activities. A deeper spiritual journey lay far in the future.

Chapter 8

The Downhill Years: 1967-1987

CHANGING CAREERS

O N JULY 1, 1967 I ARRIVED AT MY NEW JOB AS ASSISTANT DIRECTOR OF STUDENT FINANCIAL AID AT CASE WESTERN RESERVE UNIVERSITY. It was a remarkable day, not only because I had a new task, but also because it was the first day of the new era created by the joining of Case Institute of Technology and Western Reserve University. It was both an exciting and somewhat uncertain time. I would be working with a new team of three financial aid officers reporting to the Director of the Office of Financial Aid. While the processes for qualifying students for financial assistance were detailed, they were not difficult to learn. I quickly gained confidence in a totally new career. The group became a cohesive team and worked well together.

One of the benefits of my new endeavor was enrolling in one free course per semester on my own time. This enabled me to earn a Master of Arts degree in American History, just for fun. I wrote a thesis on Charles Franklin Thwing, President of Western Reserve University from 1891 to 1922. Thwing was an ordained Congregational minister who served churches in Boston and Minneapolis before arriving in Cleveland. He wrote numerous books on higher education and was a significant figure in American higher education.

After three years and a half in the Financial Aid office, I was asked to consider taking on the task of developing a unified alumni program for the merged university. It was a large mistake to think that I could be successful in such a role with no prior experience administering an alumni relations program. Even so, I said "yes" to the offer in October of 1970. In a few short months, having had no managerial experience in large, hierarchical organizations, I made enough mistakes to be told I needed to find other employment. I was able to do so fairly quickly.

St. Lawrence University

Fortunately, the contacts I had made with financial aid officers in several colleges led to an opening in the development staff at St. Lawrence University in Canton, New York. College funds development was the sort of position I had hoped for when I first considered leaving parish ministry. I felt fund raising for higher education was a worthy alternative to parish ministry, because it involved asking people to support an important mission, namely education. Before I knew anything about Case Western Reserve University, one spring day in 1967, I visited with G. T. Smith, the Vice President for Development at my alma mater, the College of Wooster. I wanted to learn about college fund raising. He gave me a copy of a new book on the art of fund raising. It was written by Harold J. Seymour and was titled *Designs for Fund-Raising*. It became a classic in the field. My host suggested I read it, and then we would have more conversations. I was very taken with what I learned about philanthropic fundraising. I still have the well-worn book on my shelf. As it worked out, I was hired at Case Western Reserve before an opportunity in college development was available. Four years later, I learned of the position at St. Lawrence and applied.

Now, in September 1971, I was in a position I had hoped for years earlier. It felt good to be back in higher education. The primary assignment was to write proposals to foundations, seeking support of projects on the campus. In the early 1970s, St. Lawrence University was engaged in a large capital campaign and focusing on developing projects related to its distinctive location north of the Adirondacks in the valley of the St. Lawrence River and in close proximity to Canada. In addition, the nearby Akwesasne Native American reservation provided opportunities for research and service projects which needed to be supported through grants. These projects were part of a major capital campaign for faculty support and endowment development. It was invigorating to work with members of the faculty, the vice president and the dean in preparing proposals to foundations and grant makers. This was the beginning of an involvement in fundraising and development that was to last for the next twenty-nine years, including several years of consulting with churches following retirement.

COUNTRY PLEASURES

Our years in St. Lawrence County included memorable experiences. We were living in an historic house six miles from the Town of Canton. Located on an old farm, the first section of the house was built in 1816 and its addition in 1890. Local histories of St. Lawrence County included an artist's rendering of what was known in the 19th century as the Butterfield Farm. In much of the 20th century it was operated as a dairy farm. A year or so before we purchased the place, the large barn with the ramp to the second-floor hay mow fell victim to neglect. In the years after the end of dairy farming, a natural spring which fed water to the cattle stalls overflowed and gradually undermined the barn's support posts. On a bitterly cold winter night before we bought the place, the barn, laden with snow, collapsed into a pile of broken timbers and splintered roofing. It was the end of what had been one of the grand dairy barns in the Town of Pierrepoint. Because it was a hazard, we had the volunteer fire department help us burn the rubble and bury the ashes and rusted, useless nails from the roof.

In succeeding years, the neighboring farmers grew corn and hay on the larger fields. One elderly farmer still used a team of horses to pull his mechanical oscillating sidebar mower to cut hay in the smaller meadow beyond the little brook not far from the backyard. Each summer, he put a few bales of hay in the old implements barn which still stood not far from the house. Our young sons transformed the stack of bales into a fort and a place to hide. One of them even raised rabbits in a hutch we built one spring and kept in that barn.

Not long after we purchased the place, we worked with the County Extension Agent to plan a farm pond just east of the house. The result was the construction of a freshwater pond in a low-lying meadow. It quickly filled with rainwater and a steady flow from a spring which was uncovered while the pond was being excavated. It was graded so that the end behind the earthen dam was ten feet deep. The pond was a welcome swimming and fishing hole in summer and an ice rink in the winter. I kept the snow off the ice with a plow mounted on our Ford tractor. Of course, the tractor only went onto the ice when it was at least eight inches thick or more. The plow blade also made it easy to pile up great mounds of snow for building snow forts. When the boys weren't learning to play hockey at the St. Lawrence University hockey rink, they were practicing their skills on our frozen pond.

The farm included about twenty acres of old trees, among them oaks, Hemlocks and old Sugar Maple trees. There also were the remnants of an old sugarhouse. It was the place where, each spring, the sap of the maples had been boiled in large, square pans heated over a continuously burning wood fire to make maple syrup. A small brook ran through the old woodlot. One year, a colony of beavers decided to build a dam and their winter house on the brook. They became a nuisance because the pond behind the dam began to encroach on the neighbor's hay meadow. The beaver mysteriously disappeared before the next winter. However, the woodlot became a wonderful hiking and camping place. Its beauty was brought home to me early one March. After tramping through the snow amid the trees on a beautiful sunny day, when the temperature was just above forty degrees, I wrote this reminiscence, titled *March in a Sleeping Sugarbush*. It appeared in the local weekly paper, the *St. Lawrence Plaindealer* under my pen name, Randy Fitz. It is reprinted here, by permission, with minor changes.

MARCH IN A SLEEPING SUGARBUSH

It was a clear crisp morning in March the first time I went into the sugarbush. It had been there, of course, since we bought the farm the previous fall. But somehow, I had not found the time to tramp through the brush and undergrowth to find the hidden secrets. Today was different. A late February thaw and quick freeze had crusted the snow. Now the maples stood dark against its white glaze. Even though the air was cold, the sun was beginning to give a suggestion of warmth. Its light and the frozen snow made it easy to wander through the trees. My footsteps made a hollow thump on the icy blanket. Occasionally a foot went through the crusted snow, breaking the woodland quiet with a sudden cracking noise, like eating peanut brittle.

Though the quiet made me think I was alone, there were others there. One by one their signs appeared. A burrow in the snow, small and round, opening from beneath some fallen branches, revealed a fox's den. And just a little farther on, the droppings of a porcupine which had clambered high into a thickly branched Hemlock revealed the presence of another winter resident. I made a mental note not to bring the dogs near its home.

The Hemlocks announced much about the age of that sugarbush. Hemlock trees usually take hold after most of the other trees have been cut for firewood or saw logs. Now they were beginning to crowd the remaining maples, holding the cold close to the ground, keeping the snow cover past the time for good sap production. The sugarbush had been asleep for a long time with winter's hibernation and from neglect as well. The trees had healed all the tap holes, left from past seasons of sugaring. Only a few rotting boards still marked where the sugaring house once stood.

But sleep is not death. It is preparation. That stand of maple trees could still give sweet sap. Hard work and good management could encourage nature's abundance. Some of the excess Hemlocks would have to be cut. Some of it could be rough sawn to build a new sugaring house. Not far from the old building site a cold stream flowed past a gap in the softening ice. It burbled with the vitality that nourishes the willows along its banks in summer. A sudden curve in the streambed brought it close to where the sugaring house had been, making it a perfect source of water for cleaning the buckets and ladles, the boiling pan and utensils used in making maple syrup.

I turned to tramp back through the trees toward the snow-covered meadow. A bit of flecked brown and gray caught my eye. I stopped to look, and there in a Hemlock, about twelve feet above the ground sat a quail. It stayed perfectly still. After watching each other for several moments, I went on. Now there was a bit more spring in my steps. The signs were there which promised that the sugarbush wouldn't sleep much longer. It was already too late to do anything about it this year. Sugaring season begins when the daytime temperature goes above freezing to about forty degrees, and the sap in the trees begins to rise. Next year I would accept nature's sweetest gift. I knew that once the first forty gallons of sap had been boiled down, the resulting gallon of syrup would be rich and smooth, the cherished light-amber quality of the first run. Next March, the sugarbush wouldn't sleep anymore.

Although there were many pleasant elements of living on a country place outside of Canton, an unrecognized cloud was lurking in the background. One aspect of college funds development involved entertaining alumni and prospective donors during cocktail receptions and social events. I was always aware on these occasions that I needed to limit the amount of alcohol I consumed. I vividly recall one occasion when too much scotch was consumed at an out-of-town event, and I found myself seriously hung-over the next morning. There were, however, occasions when excessive consumption occurred at home, more than I realized or admitted at the time, a reality I eventually came to regret.

ANOTHER MOVE

After two and a half years at St. Lawrence, I began to yearn for larger responsibilities. When the position of Executive Director of the St. Lawrence County United Way organization came open in April of 1974, I applied and ultimately was selected. This proved to be one of the most enjoyable and rewarding positions of my career. The annual campaign supported agencies in Canton, Potsdam, Ogdensburg and Messina. During my tenure, we expanded to serve previously unserved agencies in neighboring Malone in Franklin County. Sometimes, the details and challenges of the work seemed a bit overwhelming. In such moments, I took time to visit the Cerebral Palsy clinic in Potsdam, or the workshop employing individuals with handicaps. Such visits reminded me of the value of what our collective effort meant to the lives of so many people. These moments quickly put my occasional frustrations into perspective and restored my focus and resolve.

An important benefit of working with United Way was participation in the training programs of the National Academy of Volunteerism, an arm of United Way. Its week-long courses taught me key methods for engaging and empowering volunteers to work together in program development and fund-raising campaigns. The discussions provided new understandings of group processes and team building. I recognized how helpful it would have been to know these skills at the beginning of my career in the ministry. Among other insights, I saw that my desire to control outcomes had caused difficult relationships in the course of my parish ministry. The new skills proved to be extremely helpful during the later stages of my career in guiding groups to develop "buy in" for proposed programs and capital campaigns.

In the Ditch at Midnight.

Sometime in the summer of 1977 or 1978, my wife and our two sons were vacationing at her parents' cottage near Alexandria Bay, New York. I was home alone after a day at the United Way office in Canton and scheduled to attend a meeting in nearby Potsdam. While preparing dinner, I had a couple of drinks. After dinner, I drove the eight or so miles to Potsdam for the meeting. It concluded sometime after nine p.m. After the post-meeting conversations ended, I impulsively decided to stop at a nearby sports bar for a drink. I had at least two before heading home. It was after ten p.m.

Feeling lonesome as I drove toward my dark home in the country, I suddenly wanted to be with my family, approximately fifty miles away. I changed routes and turned toward the cottage at Clear Lake. About fifty miles into the trip, I was fighting increasing drowsiness. On a moonless night, the road was dark and somewhat curvy, following a small river near the town of Huevelton, New York. To my left, the river ran fairly close to the road. As I drove, drowsiness won out, and I drifted into sleep. Suddenly, I heard banging and scraping of metal on metal as the car bounced and banged out of control before jerking to a halt. It had edged off the road to the right, grinding along a steel guard rail that led the car into a wooded ditch. It ended up between a large rock on the passenger's side and a tree close to the driver's door.

The bouncing of the car going into the ditch, along with the horrible metallic scraping, jolted me awake. I was both disoriented and frightened. As I began to focus, I realized that the dome light of the car was on. The sudden stop killed the engine. Now fully awake, and still belted in my seat, I began to get my bearings. The driver's door was sprung partially open, just far enough to give me room to get out of the car. I turned off the dome light, pocketed the keys and edged my way out of the driver's side. Although the door was partially blocked by the tree, I could get through.

There were no nearby lights. Working my way out of the trees and back to the edge of the road, my night vision began to focus on the night sky. All was quiet. Thousands of stars shone overhead. In the distance, I could see the night glow of Heuvelton, a small farm town maybe a mile away. I needed to find a pay telephone in order to call for help. Cell phones didn't exist in 1978. After an hour of walking the winding star-lit road along the river, I found a pay telephone booth under a streetlight at the edge of town. It was beside the driveway to a gas station. I had no coins, but I could dial "O" and reach an operator. I told her I needed to reach my family and asked that she place a collect call to my wife. Fortunately, the number of the cottage was included in my small pocket directory of needed phone numbers.

It was now well after midnight. When my very sleepy and anxious wife answered, I told her what happened. She was not happy. I assured her I was not hurt and asked her to come and get me. I told her I was going to call the state police to report the accident, which I did. I could not leave my wrecked car in the ditch unexplained.

It was not long before the state police arrived. I described what had happened. They asked whether I had been drinking. I acknowledged I had had drinks earlier in the evening. While I was being interviewed, my wife arrived with our two sons who were asleep in the back seat. The officers asked me to lead them to the scene. They found the car. I assured them I would arrange for a tow truck to retrieve it, which I did the next day. Satisfied that I had provided accurate information, and that I had a way home, they allowed me to leave with my wife. No summons was issued. We arrived at the cottage sometime after two in the morning. Later, I was told by a person in my office that there was a brief mention of my accident on the early morning radio news in nearby Ogdensburg, but it was not repeated later in the day.

The result of this wreck was more than an embarrassment to my family and the cost of replacing a wrecked car. My insurance agent asked what had happened. My answer was that I had fallen asleep at the wheel, which was true. He didn't ask about, and I did not mention, the consumption of alcohol. Because the state police did not issue a summons, no points were marked on my driving record. The deeper, more damaging outcome was that this episode did not cause me to see that I had a serious problem with alcohol. It would be several years before I confronted that reality.

For several months, stresses had been developing in our marriage. That same summer, Karen and I agreed to see a counselor associated with one of the nearby colleges. After several sessions, both jointly and separately, the counselor apparently felt I was the person in need of therapy more than my wife, but he did not say so directly to me. My wife withdrew from counseling. After one or two more sessions with me, the therapist announced that because the new academic year was about to begin, he could not continue sessions with me. He did not offer a referral to another therapist. I don't recall that he ever brought up the issue of addiction to alcohol. I didn't.

More Life Changes

In the fall of 1978, I was invited to apply for a position in the Fund-raising Division of United Way of America and ultimately was hired. I started work on January 1, 1979. The task was to help develop and write guidebooks on aspects of fundraising. The new job necessitated a move to Alexandria, Virginia. We took our two sons with us on a house hunting-trip which also involved searching for the high school they would attend. We specifically made appointments to visit three high schools so that the boys could have a tour and meet a counselor at each school. Ultimately, they chose Mt. Vernon High School in Fairfax County. We found a home a block from the school. Their choice proved to be a happy one. Our older son, entering his junior year of high school, found real pleasure in working with the Audio/Visual department, dealing with sound systems and support for student plays. The younger son became active in dramatics and often held leading roles.

Several months after arriving in Alexandria, I began to join colleagues occasionally for after-work libations. Initially, these stops were infrequent and were cleared with my wife. Later, they became more frequent, and too often without checking in at home. On such occasions, voices were raised when I arrived late for dinner, and I became both defensive and apologetic. I continued to assert that I was in control.

In June of 1981, two and a half years after arriving at United Way of America, I was let go, along with several others, supposedly in a restructuring of departments. Once again, I faced the grieving and self-doubt of a lost job. However, having recovered from similar experiences more than once in the past, I began networking and interviewing again. This was somewhat easier because I was given sixty days of lead time and was permitted to use my office to work on the search. Fortunately, the process was not long.

In August of 1981, I began a new position as the Director of Resource Development with the District of Columbia Chapter of the American Red Cross. This was my sixth job in eleven years. It lasted almost five years, one of the two longest tenures in my career. I enjoyed the work and felt productive. My pattern of drinking in the evening, but still going to work every day, continued. However, this job also ended after the chapter manager retired and a new manager replaced me and another person early in 1986.

THE CRISIS

It was during my tenure at the Red Cross that the deepest crisis of my life began. In the fall of 1983, I became a volunteer in a local political campaign. Several weeks later, I met a woman who had been a long-time volunteer in local political circles. Earlier in the year she had separated from her husband. I was drawn to her activism and positive personality. She was in the process of divorcing. I began finding reasons to meet her, and the relationship grew beyond simple friendship. By late spring of 1984, amid great pain, I admitted the affair. It was not my first inappropriate relationship. Infidelity had occurred in the past, been discovered and then patched over without professional help. Now, I agreed to try therapy with my wife, but I was half-hearted and not really committed to it. I briefly saw a therapist who tried to get me to acknowledge I had a problem with alcohol. I continued to deny it. After a few sessions, I stopped the counseling. Deeply conflicted between wanting the new relationship and feeling guilt over my actions, I moved out of our home.

Sometime after it became known that Karen and I were separated, I received a letter written by her mother. It conveyed the hurt and pain my parents-in-law felt at the breakup of our marriage. She expressed to me the fact that both she and her husband had been deeply distressed by the behavior caused by my drinking. I was amazed, and felt shamed by the expression of their love for me she conveyed with their hope that, with God's help, I would one day find myself. At the time I received that letter, I accepted its message of pain and hurt, but put the letter away with others. It went forgotten for decades until I found it again about three years ago. Several years after her letter, an amazing resolution to this brokenness took place.

Over several months of living apart from Karen, I could not decide what to do. I continued the new relationship, but it began to be strained. My drinking pattern continued. Frustrated with my indecision, the woman with whom I was so deeply involved delivered an ultimatum. One day, she simply said to me: "I don't want to see you anymore. Don't call me. You can't decide whether you want to be with me, or you want to try to repair your marriage." It hurt a lot to hear these words, and I knew the relationship was ruptured.

I decided to try to stop drinking. In the summer of 1985, I managed to stay dry for six weeks by doing what is known in addiction recovery circles as "white knuckling it." The phrase means hanging on for dear life while trying not to succumb to the urge to drink. In September, I was sent by the Red Cross to Florida to team up with another Red Cross staff person to mount a fund-raising effort to support victims of Hurricane Elena. During this trip, I gave in to the urge for a drink in the hotel bar. Consuming one and going to bed, I convinced myself I could control the amount I drank and be OK. Within two weeks of returning to my apartment, I was back to my old level of consumption at night.

Several weeks after the ultimatum, it was clear to me that I did not want to go back to the marriage. In a painful face-to-face conversation, I told my estranged wife. I also realized that even if this meant I had to live as much as ten years or more as a single person, I was prepared for that possibility. I had no idea whether there ever could be any chance for restarting the now-disrupted relationship I had been told to leave.

After more than a month with no contact, Ginny, the woman who had been my new love, called and asked me to retrieve several possessions I had left behind. A week or ten days after doing so, I ventured a phone call asking if she would meet me for coffee. She agreed. During that call, I acknowledged I did not want to try to recover my marriage. I would be the one to seek a divorce. Over time other conversations occurred. We began to see each other again.

The Christmas season in 1985 was the loneliest period of my life. The only real recollection I have of that season centers around the single small poinsettia plant I bought and placed on a low mahogany chest I used as a coffee table. The small pot was wrapped in red foil. I watered it occasionally, but unknowingly, I overdid the watering on one occasion. This produced an ugly water stain underneath the plant which I didn't discover until the plant finally faded and lost its red leaves. When I discarded it, I found the water stain on the chest. It stayed there several years until I finally sanded and refinished the top of the chest.

The memory of that plant and the stain it produced still reminds me each holiday season that there are many people for whom the holidays are a lonely and very difficult time. I appreciate the fact that many churches hold a special Blue Service to acknowledge people for whom Christmas and the holidays are emotionally painful.

In late October and November, Ginny and I continued to see each other. Through the winter, the breakup between us was mending. We began attending church together. Early in 1986, the manager of the Red Cross chapter retired. The new manager wanted new people in several positions. Again, I faced a job change. In April, I accepted a job with the foundation associated with a nearby hospital. Over the summer, the relationship with Ginny deepened. Our interests were very much alike. She was intensely involved as a volunteer in political campaigns, and I also attended events with her. She was chair of the local Democratic committee more than once. At most political campaign receptions in private homes alcohol was available. My use continued, and consumption varied from moderation to excessive, particularly on weekends. Ginny seemed able to maintain moderation. We did not talk about alcohol use, and my drinking did not arise as an issue.

On Ginny's birthday in early August, we were engaged. Two months later, in mid-October, we married in a modest ceremony. It was attended by her family members and a modest number of invited friends. My parents were present, and Dad assisted the minister of our church in performing the ceremony. The reception was held the next day, and we did not serve alcohol. By their presence, my parents granted me their love and support through the events of my divorce and remarriage. Ginny and I soon would face an unexpected reality.

My "Morning After"

In January of 1987, barely three months into our new marriage, a family member entered treatment for alcohol addiction. In February, we joined other parents in a required week of family therapy for parents. We were there to learn about the nature of addiction. Alcoholism is called a family disease, not only because of the addicted member's illness, but also because of the ways in which family members become enablers of its progression and victims of the family dysfunction which happens as a result.

While attending the week of family therapy, my wife and I were staying at a bed and breakfast. On the second evening, we had dinner in a comfortable restaurant nearby. It offered warmth and relaxation after a long and intense day. The lighting in the restaurant was set at a soft, calming glow. The tableware and linen tablecloth suggested a style and tradition of permanence one doesn't find with stainless steel utensils and paper placemats.

The waiter was attentive, but unobtrusive. After a polite greeting and welcome, he asked if we would like something from the bar. Ginny ordered her usual wine. I ordered my favorite drink, scotch on the rocks with a splash of water. The conversation was light and easy, reviewing the day's activities. When the waiter took our dinner order, we ordered a second round. After our leisurely dinner, contrary to my usual practice, I ordered an after-dinner drink and finished the evening with a second. Ginny was surprised by my consumption of two after-dinner drinks. She remarked about the fact that I usually didn't do after-dinner drinks, but said no more.

The next morning, after an ample breakfast, we headed to the third day of family sessions. We were participating in educational sessions about the nature of addiction as well as conversations about issues involved with our family member, in our case, a teenager. On this day, the group was seated in a circle. Each person was asked to say his or her first name and to indicate their involvement in the situation of the family member in treatment. The usual introduction went something like, "Hi, my name is So-and-so, and I am co-dependent." This is a term which essentially means the person is impacted both emotionally and in specific ways by their family member's addiction. One or two members of the group added the fact that they also were in recovery, primarily from alcohol.

When my turn came, I said, "Hi. I'm Rob. I'm co-dependent, and … I'm an alcoholic." There was a brief moment of absolute quiet. And then my wife's familiar voice, blurted out: "Oh s--, I've done it again!" As uncomfortable laughter rose from the group, I heard her say "You didn't tell me you were going to do this." She went on to explain to the group that her former husband had been an alcoholic. Once again, she was confronted with the reality of an addicted spouse.

In the course of the previous two days, I had become undeniably aware that, for a long time, I had not been able to control my drinking. When I got up that morning, the possibility of acknowledging I was addicted was the farthest thing from my mind. As individuals acknowledged the truth of their involvement with this disease, I was compelled to face honestly the reality of my own addiction. I was almost as surprised to hear my words as Ginny was. Later, it occurred to me that my two after-dinner drinks the night before were my unconscious kiss-off to the drug that had caused me untold moments of embarrassment and dysfunction for so many years. Today, I choose to say, "I am powerless over alcohol," or, on some occasions, "I'm allergic to it." **This event, *My Morning After,* was the moment of my spiritual rebirth and the beginning of my journey toward physical and emotional recovery.**

When I got home from the family therapy week on Friday, I called Paul, the person whose phone number a friend had given me five years earlier. I told him I needed help. The next Monday morning, President's Day 1987, I attended my first AA meeting with Paul as my sponsor. Today, after more than thirty years of living in recovery, my wife and I have an occasional laugh over the February morning in 1987 when she blurted out the now-humorous exclamation, "Oh s---, I've done it again!" Except this time the outcome has been vastly and wonderfully different for both of us. However, on that fateful morning, I could not know the many pathways I would need to travel. The most difficult part, confronting depression and profound grief and remaking my life through the discovery of my childhood trauma, would not occur until twenty-two years after I got sober.

There is an important follow-up element to my sobriety story. Three years after I re-married, having asked for and received their permission to do so, we visited my former parents-in-law at their home. Among other reasons, I wanted to acknowledge the hurt I had caused. But the response I received moved me to tears. Although he could not speak, and was paralyzed on one side from a stroke, my former father-in-law navigated his wheelchair to the door leading down to the basement of their home, the location of his woodshop. It was a place I knew well, one where he often shared his wisdom with me. Unable to speak, he pointed to Ginny and then to the door and nodded to me to take her down to see the shop. To me, this was the most profound act of forgiveness I could have experienced. It forever imprinted on my heart the meaning of unconditional love and forgiveness. Even after he died, for years my former mother-in-law continued to send me birthday cards. These two people, with whom I had been very close for more than twenty years, were more ready and able to forgive me than I have been able to forgive myself for the hurt I caused. It was a gift beyond price.

Earlier, I described the connections between the psychological damage caused by my childhood trauma and the acting-out behaviors of addiction, infidelity and depression. The reality of these connections does not alter the fact that I was and am responsible for my behaviors. I have deep regret that they are part of my life story, and for the hurt I caused many people. Making amends, wherever I could, has been part of my work of recovery.

Life does not immediately become less challenging following a decision to seek sobriety. The everyday challenges are still there. For me, another job change became necessary as the year progressed. In spite of having to face that prospect again, the benefits of not drinking began to be felt. My senses became much more attuned to the world around me. Colors were brighter. Sounds were clearer. I heard birds sing in the morning, and I began to feel physically better.

One of the major effects of addiction is the impairment of one's ability to be aware of emotions, both in one's self and in others. Slowly, as I attended AA meetings and the effects of alcohol began to leave my system, including the center of the brain which controls emotions, I started to be more attuned to what others were saying and feeling. Over time new career opportunities arose, and I began to feel a renewed sense of direction and purpose. These new ventures became some of the most meaningful and rewarding experiences of my life. They are the next chapter in the story.

Chapter 9

New Vitality, New Ministries:

1987 and Beyond

FOLLOWING THE FAMILY THERAPY SESSIONS DEALING WITH ADDICTION RECOVERY, I ATTENDED SEVERAL MEETINGS OF ALCOHOLICS ANONYMOUS EACH WEEK. Gradually, I got used to not drinking, although it took me a while to get over being angry that I could no longer enjoy the taste of scotch. Even though I was living into sobriety, the next eight years were a time of job loss and re-employment.

September of 1987 took me to a new job with the United Way of Chattanooga, Tennessee. It lasted three years, followed by four years at Mary Washington College in Fredericksburg, Virginia when a new vice president wanted someone else in my job.

There were two rewarding experiences in Chattanooga. The first was a contribution to the wider community. In Washington, I had been a long-time member of the local chapter of the National Society of Fund-Raising Executives, now known as the Association of Fund-Raising Professionals. I discovered that a number of the directors of development in non-profit organizations in Chattanooga were interested in forming a chapter. The response to the idea was substantial, and the new chapter quickly grew to include members from north Georgia as well as the Chattanooga area. I was privileged to serve as its first president. Among its contributions to the philanthropic community in Chattanooga, the chapter organized the first Fund-raising Day in the city to recognize individuals and companies which had made significant contributions to the advancement of philanthropy. Ms. Sandy Fauriol, who had been the director of fundraising for the Vietnam Veterans Memorial in Washington, D.C. was the invited keynote speaker. The celebration of Fund-Raising Day became an annual recognition event.

My second pleasure was our purchase of our first boat. Ginny and I became members of the United States Coast Guard Auxiliary. We learned a lot about boating safety from classes and direct experience as crew members on safety patrols. An essential lesson came from one of our own outings. It also was a somewhat frightening episode.

On a bright sunny day in October of 1989, we set out on a cruise in our eighteen-foot Sea Ray boat, a boat with open-air seats up front. Although we were new boaters, we had training in boat handling and basic navigation. About ten o'clock on a Saturday morning, we departed from our marina about two miles above the Chickamauga Dam on the Tennessee River. Our destination was a crafts festival several miles downriver. At the dam, we radioed the lock master for permission to lock through on the down-bound passage. After properly securing the boat to the floating restraint in the side of the lock, the water was released through the out-flow pipes. We descended safely to the lower level. When the lock gates opened, we re-started the engine and floated out along with a dozen other boats headed downriver.

We arrived at the festival after an hour of pleasant cruising. It was set up in a tree-shaded state park and featured displays of hand-made crafts, colorful quilts, wooden nick-knacks, and endless quantities of homemade pastries, jellies and foodstuffs. There were exhibits of old farm machinery, as well as hand tools and a working blacksmith's forge.

The afternoon wore on, and too soon we needed to start back. While planning the trip, I had neglected to account for the speed of the river current. Returning, the boat had to push against the current. It was stronger than usual after several rainy days. Even though we started with a full tank of gas, the falling gas gauge began to worry me.

The sun was nearing the horizon, and dusk was not far away. I knew we should get gas before we slowed down to pass upriver through Chickamauga lock. But to my dismay, no marinas appeared before we reached the lock. Night fell and my anxiety rose. At that moment, I remembered a marina just above the dam on the starboard (right) shore. We floated out of the lock on the north side of dam. To my surprise and increasing worry, the anticipated marina was dark. The moonless night made the river equally dark. I wondered if we would get to our marina before we ran out of gas.

At night, it is necessary to navigate by the lighted and unlighted reflector buoys in the river. When upbound, toward the source of a river, the red buoys must be kept to the mariner's starboard, or right, side. The green must be on the port, or, left, side. The lighted buoys are fairly far apart. Between them, the colored metal buoys are visible in the night only if a spotlight or strong flashlight picks the colored reflectors out of the darkness.

A couple of miles upriver, as we neared the bright lights surrounding the nuclear power plant, I could see the red warning lights blinking atop the steel power transmission towers on either bank. As we cruised between the towers and continued upriver, I forgot that the river took a bend to the left. Suddenly, in the dimming light of the power plant behind us, I saw a small buoy pass on my left side. To my astonishment, it was reflecting red! What was it doing on the left? It was supposed to be on the right. The basic rule of navigation, "Red right returning," still applied. It dawned on me that we were headed for the right-hand shore as the river bent to the left. We were about to run aground!

The beam of the powerful flashlight quickly found the green buoy, and I made the required course correction to return to the channel. We were close to our marina and made it back safely to the nearest dock. Using the flashlight as our only light, we secured the boat and went home. Upon returning the next day, we were startled by the fact that the engine would not start. Using a long length of line (nautical term for rope), we literally pulled the boat by hand around to the gas dock. The moral: do not break the mariners' rule for fuel consumption. Use one third out, and one third back, with one third in reserve when you get home. That, and a spare two-gallon can of gas for insurance will get you through almost any situation. We were members of the Coast Guard Auxiliary for more than two decades.

Our three years in Chattanooga were especially important to us. Dad and Mom had moved to a retirement community called Uplands. It was eighty miles north, in Pleasant Hill, Tennessee on the Cumberland Plateau. Many of the retirees were retired ministers and former missionaries. Some were folks from other parts of the country whom my parents had known over the years. Others were local people whose lives were rooted in Tennessee. One couple were dear friends who had been college classmates in the nineteen twenties. We were able to celebrate birthdays and holidays with Mom and Dad from Thanksgiving in 1987 through the holidays in 1989. But sadness came when Dad was diagnosed with lung cancer in November of 1989. He lived four months and died on March 6, 1990. His death affected me deeply, as I have described elsewhere. Afterward, Mom continued to live in the home she and Dad built in 1973. Eventually, she moved to an assisted living apartment and spent the last years of her life in the nursing home. She died in April 2000 at age ninety-two.

My work experience in Chattanooga was not going well. I began the search for a new opportunity. This led to accepting a job as Assistant Director of Development at Mary Washington College in Fredericksburg, Virginia. It was a delight to be working again on a college campus. My time there lasted a little less than four years.

One of my pleasant duties was to help staff and host the 50th reunion classes. Mary Washington was a women's college before it became co-educational in the early 1970s. The planning committees I worked with were comprised of female graduates from the 1940s. They taught me a lot about the antics of college women in those days! They had their ways of circumventing the rules of *in loco parentis* which were in vogue in the 1940s. It was surprising to learn from an alumna that one such rule required prospective dates to meet the approval of the Dean of Women. Students also found ways to circumvent rules about smoking and were skilled at returning to campus undetected after the curfew. How times have changed!

About a year after Dad died, I drove from Fredericksburg to Pleasant Hill to check on Mom. On the way, I passed a newly disked field with its freshly-turned rows of warm brown earth, ready to be planted. My grandfathers saw such fields. I wondered if future generations would have the same opportunity. This poem was the result.

FURROWS IN SPRINGTIME

Passing by a freshly disked field,
The warm brown furrows
Ready to receive their planting,
Reminds me of Ohio boyhood
Passing newly-tilled fields and
Hearing Dad speak of
Uncle John and the farm.

Now Dad is no longer here,
But returned to earth,
As when Bromfield of Malabar Farm*
Wrote of living connected to the earth,
His ashes, at the last,
Befriending its eternal embrace.

Together, we are bound
In the cycle of this earth's life,
So that in our living and dying,
We are linked to the next generation.

Yet wonder asks whether, in coming years,
Our living will so contaminate fragile earth
That dying will be permanent,
And future generations decease before birth,
Never to know
Warm brown furrows in springtime?

*Louis Bromfield's Malabar Farm was devoted to simple methods of organic farming in the 1920s. Its principles enabled Bromfield to restore an exploited barren tract to productivity.

The Vice President of Development who hired me left Mary Washington College three and half years after I arrived. Three months into his tenure, the new Vice President decided he wanted to choose the occupant of my position. Once again, I faced a job search. It resulted in two and a half years of networking. I was able to find part-time work for more than a year and a full-time assignment during the last six months of 1996.

OPPORTUNITY KNOCKS

While this search process was going on, the thought crossed my mind that it might be fun to start to work on a Doctor of Ministry degree. This is the highest professional degree for clergy in my denomination. It is intended to give ministers an opportunity for further study and growth after a number of years out of seminary. Even though I was not actively serving a congregation, I was encouraged to apply. My wife supported the idea. To help out, my church agreed to provide partial support for tuition in return for several hours a month working with the committee charged with organizing the annual giving campaign. I began the course work in the summer session of 1995. By Christmas of 1996, I finished the required course work, and had the research and writing of the dissertation to do.

About midway through my time at Mary Washington, we bought a two-acre wooded lot on Mason Neck, near the Potomac River in Fairfax County. We planned to build a home on a portion of the lot. Because I was not working, the dream house was postponed. However, a number of tall pine trees stood on the lot, a portion of which had been blown partly over in a windstorm. I set about clearing them. On a beautiful Saturday morning in the fall of 1995, fatigued from woodcutting, I sat on a stump just watching sunlight dance on the autumn color in a nearby tree. An occasional squirrel rummaged in the dry leaves on the ground. A blue jay screeched in the distance. The only other sound was the occasional soft murmur of a gentle breeze high in the pines.

Lost in the stillness and the wonder of the moment, I was imagining what sort of work I would like for one more job before retiring. In a prayer-like frame of mind, the words to God formed. "Before I retire, I would like to run a non-profit agency, preferably related to the church in some way. I want it to be in New England, a place I really love." Once again, memories of my childhood in Connecticut and the seminary years in New Haven flooded back. It was a wistful sort of prayer and reverie. It soon faded, and I went back to my labors.

Several months later, in the summer of 1996, our home phone rang. The caller was the port chaplain in Portland, Maine. He explained that he was one of the staff members working with merchant seafarers on behalf of the Boston Seaman's Friend Society. The Society was seeking a new Executive Director. My name was suggested to him by the pastor of Prides Corner Congregational Church near Portland. Five years earlier, she had been the associate pastor at our home church in Annandale, Virginia. After sharing information about the Society's work in ministering to merchant sailors, the caller asked if I wished to be considered for the Executive Director's position. The role involved overall management of the Society and its chaplains in the ports of Boston; Portland, Maine and Portsmouth, New Hampshire. I agreed to be considered. After several interviews and a visit to Boston, I was appointed, as of January 1, 1997. Since Ginny was working for the State of Virginia and needed to protect her retirement, I arranged to stay at the Society's lodging and office facility. I began commuting on the US Airways shuttle from Washington to Boston every other Monday morning.

Installation by Boston Seaman's Friend Society

Later in the year, on Sunday afternoon, November 9, Boston was under a drizzling rain from a low-hanging misty, gray sky. The glorious New England autumn colors long since had fallen to the ground. Now, they were ugly, brown sodden clumps of dead leaves littering the streets and walkways, serving as slippery hazards for pedestrians and vehicles alike. In spite of the sour weather, this was to be an afternoon of celebration. Slowly, friends and colleagues were arriving for a special event at the storied Boston Navy Yard, now known as the Charlestown Navy Yard. The occasion was my formal installation as the Executive Director of the Boston Seamen's Friend Society, an historic maritime ministry founded in 1827 to serve merchant seamen who labored aboard the merchant sailing ships calling in Boston Harbor. To be relevant to today's world, the board adopted a shortened doing-business-as name and is now known in the maritime community as Seafarer's Friend.

Participants were gathering for the installation service which was held in the stately brick and white mansion located on the high ground at the head of the Boston Navy Yard. Built in 1805 to be the Commandant's House, it offers a wide view of the piers and facilities of this storied shipyard. It is one of the birthplaces of America's naval history. From inside the tall, arched windows of this elegant house, one had a view of USS *Constitution* moored at its pier, its elegant stern rising above the waters of its berth. A trim white dory hung in davits above a golden eagle, ready for use should *Constitution* have occasion to put to sea. Meanwhile, her tall masts, yardarms and lines of the rigging offered an imposing silhouette against the gloomy November sky.

Inside the Commandant's House, the day was brightened by an attractive reception prepared in the dining room adjacent to the front parlor. A large bouquet of red carnations interspersed with tiny white baby's breath drew one's eye to the center of the table. A white sheet cake, appropriately decorated with flourishes of "ecclesiastical red" and an inscription in red frosting, the primary color for formal church-related ceremonies, marked the occasion. It was the center piece of a formally set table prepared for the reception to follow the service. Red and multicolored vestments worn by clergy participants in the service added to the celebratory atmosphere.

As the appointed hour for the service approached, a modest congregation comprised of the Society's board members, friends, and members of area congregations of the United Church of Christ quieted in anticipation. After a word of welcome from the president of the board of directors, the service opened with an Invocation and a hymn. The text for the sermon was Psalm 107, verses 23-31. They speak of the wonder and peril of those whose livelihood comes from seafaring.

23 "...Some went down to the sea in ships.
   doing business on the mighty waters;
24 they saw the deeds of the Lord,
   his wondrous works in the deep.
25 For he commanded and raised the stormy wind,
   which lifted up the waves of the sea.
26 They mounted up to heaven, they went down to the depths;
   their courage melted away in their calamity;
27 they reeled and staggered like drunkards,
   and were at their wits' end.
28 Then they cried to the Lord in their trouble,
   and he brought them out from their distress.
29 he made the storm be still,
   and the waves of the seas were hushed.
30 Then they were glad because they had quiet,
   and he brought them to their desired haven.
31 Let them thank the Lord for his steadfast love,
   for his wonderful works to humankind..."

The Reverend Doctor James Crawford, the Senior Minister at the Old South Church on Copley Square in Boston, rose to deliver the sermon. Standing six feet-four inches tall with a shock of white hair, he provided a commanding voice and presence, riveting our attention. His sermon title was: *In the Eye of the Hurricane.* For his primary illustration, he drew upon the writing of Professor Philip Hallie, who taught philosophy at Wesleyan University in Connecticut in the years after the Second World War. Dr. Crawford outlined his story. Born in Chicago, Hallie grew up in a tough neighborhood, and was bullied and ostracized because he was a Jew. Later, he came to believe that evil always triumphed in the end. His experiences in France during the second world war only re-enforced his conviction.

Later, he began a study of the Holocaust. What he discovered deepened his cynicism, convincing him that goodness had no chance of triumphing.

At the depth of his despair, Philip Hallie happened upon a narrative of the heroism of the people in the French village of Le Chambon-Sur-Lignon. Reading of their heroic efforts to stand up to Nazis and the Vichy regime, the tears begin to flow down his cheeks as he learned of the efforts of this Huguenot village to hide, care for and provide hospitality to 5,000 German, Dutch, and French Jews who sought refuge during the devastation of Europe and the genocide against a whole class of people. Learning of this enormous act of courage and hospitality, Hallie began a search for other examples of profound hospitality and care for strangers carried out under violent and harsh circumstances in order to help, heal and save.

As he explored these new-found examples of extravagant welcome of refugees and strangers under dire circumstances, Hallie struggled to find a metaphor which would describe the essence of the experiences he found. It came to him in the summer of 1979 when hurricane Gloria smashed into the east coast. Hallie and his family were caught in their home as the storm hit, shattering doors and windows, flooding the basement. They huddled against the storm as it raged. And then, suddenly, the fury subsided. Hallie found himself gazing at blue sky and hearing birds sing. The family was grouped together holding hands, hiding from the storm. Crawford reported Hallie's observations:

> [We] were in the eye of the hurricane. The four
> of us kept holding each other's hands for a while,
> but now there was a surprising gentleness in
> our feelings. Our feelings of terror had become
> feelings of tenderness toward one another and
> toward the world outside our kitchen. Then and
> there, I realized that the peace I had found in Le
> Chambon was like this. Peace sometimes stands
> like the eye of a hurricane in the very middle of
> power...The ethically pure Chambonais, who did
> not hate or kill in order to help life thrive, pushed

back the walls of the eye of the hurricane, until
the murderous winds seemed so far away as to be
unreal…

Crawford observed: "Pushing back the walls of the Hurricane's eye! In a world where hospitality is hard to come by, where courage is frequently in short supply, where spontaneous caring and mutual responsibility is something before which we stand in awe, this Seaman's Friend Society, as I read the story, appears as a witness amid the eye of the hurricane." Crawford's words ring true in current-day America.

When the sermon and Charge to the Minister, outlining the work to which I had been called, were concluded, I felt both honored and humbled to have been welcomed into the company of a long heritage of chaplains and executive directors of this historic Society. It had been founded by very famous and tenacious ministers in Boston who were concerned about the spiritual and moral well-being of merchant sailors. In purchasing a hotel for sailors, they established a Bethel, or house of God, as a safe sanctuary amidst the bars and brothels of the Boston waterfront. Thus they, together with the churches, made the effort to lessen the hardships and dangers which were the daily risks in the lives of seafarers.

This Service of Installation that day more than twenty years ago represents for me one of the clear moments when God granted me grace and reconciliation. Much of my life has been a struggle to push back the walls of my own metaphorical hurricane. It has been a search for emotional and spiritual health, including development of a personal sense of self-worth to overcome my long-held and deeply-rooted sense of unworthiness. It was a feeling of unworthiness fostered by my own failings and family expectations that were ingrained in me long before I was conscious of their presence and power.

The final words from the Rev. Dr. Crawford were in the form of a Charge to the Chaplain/Executive Director. This was the presentation to me of the mission to which I had been called. The work of the Society is to provide a presence to seafarers who visit the ports of Boston, Portsmouth and

Portland in order to lessen their loneliness and distress which arises from the very risky and sometimes lethal profession of seafaring.

The Society relies on volunteers, churches and service organizations to do its work. The center for seafarers in each port often provides transportation so that they may go ashore to shop for needed personal items and gifts to send home. Shore leave is a contractual right, but was made more complex by the strict regulations of the Department of Homeland Security following the catastrophe of September 11, 2001. Chaplains are called on at times to advocate for seafarers' rights, sometimes using the resources and help of the Center for Seafarers' Rights in New York. At other times they are asked to help resolve conflicts aboard ship. I encountered such a situation one summer evening.

DOCKSIDE DIPLOMACY

When the telephone rang about eight o'clock one evening, it roused the night manager at Seaman's House. I was reading when he came to my door to tell me a ships' agent was on the phone. The agent is the on-shore person who represents the company hired to care for provisioning the ship and taking care of on-shore relationships while the ship is in port. He wanted me to come to a ship and help resolve a dispute.

The crew of a car-carrier, known as a Ro-Ro (roll on-roll off), was refusing to sail. Apparently, a conflict came up between the Filipino deck crew and the Korean officers, specifically the Korean cook. Members of crew feared the cook might taint their food and cause illness or worse while the ship was underway to its next destination. The agent, unable to resolve the conflict, had turned to me for help.

As the evening light faded to darkness, Bill, the night manager, and I drove through the bustling night streets to the auto pier north of the Tobin Bridge. The Filipino bosun was in the doorway at the head of the gangway. With some trepidation, I headed for the narrow, springy plank which ascended from the pier to the entrance to the interior of the ship. Only a loose rope looped through three or four widely-spaced steel stakes on one side of the unsteady plank offered a bit of safety.

At the top of the gangway, I asked permission to come aboard. The bosun, a Filipino who spoke English well, consented and led me into a cavernous space inside the ship. It had been emptied of its cargo of cars. They now sat in tightly-packed rows in the fading light on the auto pier. We walked through the dimly-lit steel cavern and up flights of stairs through three more vast and empty decks to the crew quarters and a narrow hallway leading to the captain's office.

The protocol for a chaplain boarding a ship requires a visit to the captain's office to seek permission to speak to the crew. As we walked down that hallway, I noticed quantities of uncooked brown rice strewn on the deck, most of it swept to either side. A crumpled twenty-five-pound burlap rice bag lay nearby.

Arriving at the captain's office, the bosun spoke brief words to the man behind a desk, a Korean wearing a captain's uniform. I waited wordlessly during this brief exchange. Turning his attention from the bosun to me, the captain said simply: "Just want peace." He nodded his head and waved us toward the door, whereupon I was led to a crewman's cabin.

The cabin was packed with about a dozen Filipino crewmen, all looking expectantly at me and their leader. One of the Korean officers was seated in the large square recess in the outside wall which also housed a porthole. He was puffing clouds of smoke from a cigarette. With several men crammed in this small cabin, the air was both tense and stifling. My mind was racing, wondering what I had gotten into, and how in the world I was going resolve the as yet unknown issue. I later learned that the Filipino crew had asked for a port chaplain to come and assist them.

Clearly, no one wanted to talk while one of the ship's officers was present. Nor was there any way I was going to persuade the speechless smoker to leave, much less climb past a cabin full of deck crew. It occurred to me to ask the bosun to take us to another cabin. He quickly agreed. As the crew was starting to leave, the officer began to go with us. I signaled to him to stay behind. He did, and we relocated to a nearby cabin.

While we were moving, I told the bosun of my year of study in the Philippines, so long ago it was probably before he was born. He was quite surprised, but with a few words, our relationship was cemented. As soon as the door to our new location was closed, the crew began to chatter in Tagalog. After a few moments of listening, the bosun quieted them. There was some conversation back and forth before the bosun turned back to me. He explained that, after all the autos had been unloaded by the local drivers, the crew refused to sail because they feared for their safety at sea. They were afraid one of their number might be thrown overboard in retaliation for their revolt over the condition of the food on board. Such retaliation is not unknown in the maritime world. The bosun told me that the crew would agree to go back to work if I would promise to call the port chaplain in their next scheduled port. I was to ask that chaplain to go aboard when the ship arrived to be sure that nothing had happened to any of the crew while the ship was underway. I agreed to make the call, and the crew agreed to return to work.

With the situation resolved, the bosun led me back down to the gangway. More than an hour had passed since I was first there. In the interim, the tide rose and the ship with it. Now the gangway was on a much steeper incline, and looked much riskier than it appeared earlier. Peering down the length of the gangplank, I was relieved by the thought that I only had to go down it, not up. After a brief hesitation, I stepped onto the gangway and started down as rapidly as I dared, stepping on the cleats (wood strips) nailed across its width to keep me from slipping and tumbling toward the dark water between ship and pier. Once I was safely on the shore, the bosun yelled down to the ship's agent on the pier that the conflict was resolved. That evening, I called the port chaplain in the next port of call and was assured that the ship would be visited when it arrived. Relieved that my first experience with ethnic conflict on board a ship was resolved, I slept well.

COMPLETING THE DOCTOR OF MINISTRY DEGREE

The fact that I was commuting on the US Airways shuttle between home in Virginia and Seaman's House in Boston meant that I had nights and every other Saturday free. Many Sundays I visited churches to promote the work of the Society and invite financial support. For the first months, I spent my evenings immersing myself in the Society's history and current issues. Thereafter, I was able to devote significant time to developing and writing my dissertation for the Doctor of Ministry degree.

My topic was the history and use of endowments in the church, and my primary advisor was Professor Lloyd Hartley. The research included a study of how endowments were used in the early church, through the Middle Ages and the Reformation Period and into the contemporary world. A chapter dealt with Jesus' teachings on the relationship between wealth and faith. One chapter included research into how modern churches develop policies governing the use of endowed funds. In March of 1998, I defended the work, and was graduated from Lancaster Theological Seminary in May.

The new knowledge gained from this academic experience was invaluable when I was invited to serve in several part-time pastoral assignments, after I retired in May of 2000. Part-time pastoral work included serving sixteen months at Rock Spring Congregational UCC in Arlington, Virginia from October 2003 through January 2005. This assignment included periodic preaching and regular visits to several elderly members of the congregation as well as some committee work. This work was an affirmation of my call to ministry. I am deeply grateful for this return to the work to which I was first called. Over the next several years, I consulted with churches in support of their capital campaigns. These projects raised the funds to refurbish buildings, start endowments and build a new building for a church.

DRAWN TO THE SEA

While writing this memoir, it occurred to me there is a thread woven into the fabric of my life which I had not recognized until the late stages of the work. Before her illness when I was a young child, my mother took me to swimming lessons sponsored by the Red Cross at a beach on Long Island Sound. As long as I can remember, I have been drawn to boats and the sea. My first experience on a boat dates to a visit my family made to a summer cottage on Long Island Sound around the time I was eight or nine years old. The cottage belonged to our next-door neighbors. Their son, Bobby, was a year or two older than I. On this summer day, our parents let us take the rowboat for a ride.

At low tide, we could walk across the sandbar to get to the boat, floating at anchor some distance from the house. Walking across the wet sand, little waterspouts squirted from the sand when we stepped near a buried clam. We felt cool wet sand squishing between our toes. When we returned from our rowing, the tide had begun to rise. Leaving the boat riding on its anchor, we waded back through the calf-deep water to the house. Ever since, I have been drawn to oceans and great bodies of water.

Two summers after my first rowboat ride, we moved to Sandusky, located on a large bay opening into Lake Erie. Our first couple of nights were with friends whose home overlooked the lake. I still remember looking out the big bay window in the living room toward the distant horizon and seeing a plume of smoke from one of the lake freighters on the horizon as it traveled east, probably headed to Cleveland, with iron ore from Duluth for the steel mills. I was intrigued by the thought that I could see these big ships on Lake Erie. Later, in bed on the screened-in sleeping porch, the sound of gently lapping waves on the shore below whispered their own calming good night.

Sandusky was a busy port visited by the distinctive long ships, built especially for use on the Great Lakes. Long trains from southern Ohio delivered coal to the huge loaders at the docks on the west side of town. The loaders lifted an entire coal car high above the dock and tipped its contents into a large chute directed into the ship's hold. On warm summer nights, with our bedroom windows open, we could hear the coal clatter into the chute. That sound was my "coal chute lullaby." It accompanied me to sleep on the humid nights.

Fascinated with the long lake freighters, I read all the books I could find about Great Lakes shipping. The maritime history of this great inland waterway, from the days of sail to the modern era, is captivating. These specialized ships, known as "lakers," carry iron ore, coal, grain and other bulk cargoes. Their history is filled with maritime disasters and heroism.

I learned to sail in Sandusky. When I was in seventh grade, I couldn't stay away from the sailing club docks in the summer. The primary activity of the club was the twice-weekly sailing races. Being a preacher's kid, I could be at the sailing docks on Wednesday evenings, but not Sunday mornings. If the family was not doing something else, I rode my bike to the sailing club before six o'clock, hoping for a chance to be aboard one of the boats.

The docks would be busy with members of the club preparing their sails and gear for the evening race. It was important to hang out near the activity, but also to stay out from underfoot. There was an art to adopting just the right look of longing, hoping that a skipper would notice the kid silently praying that someone would ask him if he wanted to go along. If a good wind was up, every skipper would need more weight onboard for ballast.

There were two primary classes of boats, Thistles and Interlakes. Both carried a main sail and a jib. The jib is the triangular sail in front of the main sail. One evening, Mr. Caldwell, the swim coach at the high school, asked if I wanted to go along on his Interlake. I climbed aboard. I could handle the jib when the skipper called "prepare to come about."

We sailed well enough to be in the lead after two legs of the triangular course. But then the wind died to a mere soft breath and we were creeping along. Somehow, we managed to cross the finish line first. As we came past the break wall into the dock area, a sudden strong puff of wind blew up. When the blast hit us, the boat just capsized and dumped us in the water, swim-coach skipper and all! We righted the boat and, soaking wet, climbed back aboard. Coach Caldwell steered us back to the dock. As the sun set, we endured the catcalls of the skippers who lost the race. That was my sailor's baptism!

It is easy to see why the work of the Boston Seaman's Friend Society was a natural fit for me, even though I had no experience in the merchant maritime world. I can't explain the source of my life-long love of boats and the sea. Perhaps, many generations ago, it was lodged in my DNA by distant ancestors whose livelihood came from the sea. My Boston experiences answered my silent prayer quiet morning in the woods, musing about a job in New England.

One of my poems reflects some of the inspiration I gain from the sea. I have made several visits to Mystic Seaport in Connecticut. This poem is based on a painting of this 19th century harbor in late fall or early winter.

Mystic Perspectives

Standing on the quay
In the cold moonlight,
Seeing across the wharves and slips
The glow of night lamps
Through windows closed against the chilled air.
Riding in silence,
Creaking on their moorings,
Lie the darkened schooners, sloops and skiffs
Of men and boys home from the sea.
Beyond quiet shops, the dark trees,
Barren from winter's drain,
Stand mirthlessly in the moonlit night,
Taller than the rooftops
And not much taller than the masts,
Nor as high as the steeple on the green.
These are the perspectives that make the world
Human size.

First Congregational United Church of Christ, Sandusky, Ohio,
the Church Rob attended and his father served from 1947 to 1958.

First Congregational Church, United Church of Christ,
North Ridgeville, Ohio

Immanuel United Church of Christ,
Cambridge, Maryland

Rock Spring Congregational, UCC,
Arlington, Virginia

Chapter 10

Meeting the Unexpected Part II

IN FEBRUARY OF 2011, I NEEDED TO RETURN TO THERAPY, EVEN IF ONLY FOR INTERMITTENT SESSIONS. The childhood pain I felt about my relationship with Mom quickly resurfaced. I was reminded again of the photo I shared with Dr. A. near the start of therapy – the one showing a mom dropping her boys off on the first day of school and giving them a protective hug at curbside before sending them on their way. The familiar feelings were welling up again. "Why couldn't my Mom be there for me?"

Once again, Dr. A. reminded me that my Mom wasn't emotionally available to me. This was true while she was in the hospital, and it continued in varying degrees for many years afterward. In addition, Dad kept his emotions hidden. He especially did not allow expressions of anger, and we boys learned to keep our feelings to ourselves.

To help out Dad, my grandmother Caris and Mom's aunt Rachel came to Bridgeport while Mom was hospitalized and for some period after she got home. I have no recollection of their presence and no recalled feelings about their presence. Nor do I recall any reaction to my mother bringing home a new baby.

VISIT TO THE HOSPITAL

As we talked about Mom coming home, I suddenly remembered that Dad took me to the hospital to see Mom. My brother Frank went too. He was three years younger than me. Dr. A. asked: "What do you remember about going to the hospital."

I remember that Daddy took us in a different door than the front. I remember feeling that even though we were with him, kids weren't supposed to be there.

"What do you remember about being inside the hospital?"
We climbed some stairs, and walked down a long hallway.
"Do you remember your Mom's room?"

It was all white. Her bed was white. I didn't like being there.

"Do you remember talking to her?"

Not really. I just remember she was very sick. I think she was glad we were there, but I wanted to leave.

"Do you remember any other feelings you had?

I was frightened. I wanted to go home.

"Why did your Dad take you to see your Mom.?"

I think he thought she might die. Suddenly a catch in my throat, and the tears welled up. *He wanted her to see us again.*

Now, words tumbled amid flooding tears – words I'm sure I didn't say, but only felt in that long-ago moment.

I don't want Mommy to die… No! No! No! I don't want her to die. Mommy, you can't die!

It was as if I was there again. The pain was happening all over again. Once again, I needed deep gulps of air. Dr. A. instructed, "Deep breaths," and I began slowly to regain calm.

"Do you remember leaving the hospital?"

Yes. We left the same way we arrived. Back down the same stairs we had come up. I don't remember the ride home.

"What happened when you got home?"

I don't remember. I sense I went to play. Daddy and I never talked about the visit. I just pushed it away.

This was another manifestation of the long-buried trauma I suffered. Clearly the fear that my mother might die is something I heard my parents mention after I was older. I had known that Dad had taken us to the hospital, but this recalling of the experience in therapy was the first time any mental picture of the visit had come to mind. In seven decades, the intense feelings which occurred during that visit to Mom's room never came to my mind.

My brother Frank also was affected deeply by our visit. In a conversation with him in the fall of 2012, during a family gathering at Alan's home, I described my work with Dr. A. and the retelling of the hospital visit.

Frank was only three years and ten months old when the visit occurred. He told me he recalled thinking at the time that our Mom had died.

A RANGE OF ISSUES

In these renewed sessions, Dr. A. encouraged me to look at two issues, my continuing pain, regret and sense of failure over my former marriage and my belief that mine was a failed career. I did not succeed in ministry as I envisioned it in the beginning. I imagined starting in a small, rural congregation and, with each successive move, taking on a larger congregation and greater responsibility. In the early sessions with Dr. A., I realized that I was not emotionally equipped to carry the responsibilities and meet the demands of either of my congregations, one of fifty plus members, and the second of more than three hundred members.

The pattern of changing jobs every few years continued after leaving parish ministry. Sometimes the change was my choice, sometimes not. I envied my father's career in the ministry. After an initial three-year call, he served three pastorates: one of thirteen years, a second of eleven years, and the third of four years. His career was capped by ten years in a senior position in the national offices of our denomination. I idealized my Dad, and also sensed that I was competing with his career, trying to measure up to his accomplishments and to the family's expectations of professional achievement.

Dr. A. pointed out that I was continuing to view my career as unworthy, even though I have done worthwhile things along the way. In reply, I felt I was only able to do what I was required to do to keep myself together and to provide for my family. It seemed to me that most of the time, I was in a struggle to survive, interrupted by occasional periods of feeling secure.

There were elements of my career I do value. Service to United Way organizations, the Red Cross and two colleges were meaningful. I value greatly the experience as the executive director of the maritime ministry in Boston. The three interim periods serving in part-time pastoral positions are sources of satisfaction. These include being the weekend supply pastor for a year and a half in First Congregational Church in Ogdensburg, New York, during my time at St. Lawrence University. Early in retirement, from October 2003 through January 2005, I had the rewarding experience at Rock Spring Congregational UCC church. After retiring from full-time work, I spent several years serving as a consultant with several churches and institutions directing their capital campaigns. Each of these projects was a source of satisfaction and gave me opportunities to engage in ministry in a way that utilized both my theological training and my thirty years of experience in fundraising.

Still, I harbored unresolved feelings of having failed my father's expectation for my career. He never said anything about his feelings about my career other than a remark he made about my response to job changes. A few years after I left parish work, he once said to me: "You always seem to land on your feet." This was as close to praise as I ever heard him offer. However, over the years we maintained a closeness we both cherished.

After a three-month summer break, I saw Dr. A. on September 16, 2011. This was five days before the tenth anniversary of my brother Greg's death. Obviously, the sadness of losing him at age 57 was coming up. But it was more than sadness. I was angry about his dying from the effects of unchecked addiction. I was angry at all the years he lived as an unemployed person, aided by the enabling of his housemate. What sort of emotions did he experience in the course of such an existence? Or were his emotions totally anesthetized? My conversations with Dr. A. also stirred deep feelings around not wanting to see people suffer the emotionally painful consequences of their behaviors. I had known that kind of pain. I've always been sensitive to emotions in others.

My notes about three sessions in October provide the following general overview.

The work is focusing on my sense of "failure" or not measuring up to what my career dreams had been, rising to be a minister in a so called "high steeple" or large congregation. In recent sessions we have been working on helping me put aside the judgmental words about my past experience...working on enabling me to be free to experience the things I want to do – to overcome the "shoulds" and "oughts" and be able to experience the freedom to let myself be open to where my spirit leads.

The struggle with self-judgment and the recurring "down" days, the markers of returning depression, were keeping me from living as a person open to new ways of being myself.

As she worked with the habits of mind which were part of my depression, Dr. A. suggested I begin to work with a book titled *The Mindful Way through Depression: Freeing Yourself from Chronic Unhappiness*, written by Mark Williams, John Teasdale, Zindel Segal, and Jon Kabat-Zinn. It became a source which helped me start to be intentional about making changes. My next chapter, "Awaking to Awareness: Healing the Lost Boy," provides an overview of principles and practices I used to begin altering the mental habits and ruminations contributing to my depression.

At the end of 2011, I focused on concerns about my sons and their feelings and hurt at the time my marriage with their mom ended. The work was about continuing to love them and reach out to them, and to be able to let go of my own self-judgement about what is past. The older son appeared to adjust to the changes in my life as they came. He attended the simple wedding when Ginny and I were married, and he visited us after our move to Chattanooga.

For my younger son, the divorce was intensely painful. For several months he wanted no contact. He had enlisted in the Air Force and after basic training, was assigned to Langley Air Force Base near Hampton, Virginia. In spite of his emotional distance, I sent him notes anyway. Eventually I visited. Over time the relationship improved. During the intervening years since then there were visits and occasional family events with him and his wife and daughter. Now, in 2012, at Dr. A's suggestion, I went to see him again.

We spent a long time sharing our feelings. He described again how hurt he had been about my separation from the family years earlier. Again, he shared a scene from the movie *The Princess Bride* which illustrated the depth of his feeling. In it, Inigo Montoya confronts the six-fingered man who had killed Montoya's father ten years earlier. Now, the perpetrator, threatened at sword point by Montoya, pleads for his life: "I'll give you anything you want." Montoya, in obvious pain and grief, replies: "You S.O.B! I want my father back!" In that moment in the movie, my son said, his vision of the six-fingered man "was replaced by a man-sized bottle of booze, complete with three Xs across its front." I could only let the tears flow for both of us until words returned. As many times as he has seen the movie since that first encounter in 1987, the vision has never recurred. Today, we are restored. Although the times we are together are not frequent, we are no longer estranged.

2012

In early January of 2012, my work with Dr. A. turned again to the core issue that is still haunting me, the thought that, somehow, I am not acceptable, that I am not okay. Dr. A. was clear that this is not something that stems from events in my adult experiences. It ties back to some long-ago experience in my childhood. The night after this discussion, I woke from a horrible nightmare. The essence of it follows:

> I was captive in a strange place, restrained on a
> gurney and screaming for someone to come and free
> me from a hideous ghost – a women all in gold – who
> laughed hysterically at me. I kept swinging at her,
> trying to hit her, but my hand only went through the
> vapor of her appearance as if she was a mirage. I
> began screaming a person's name, one I don't recall,
> hoping for rescue when my wife sharply yelled at me

to waken.

After I regained some composure, I remembered that, before bed, I was going through thoughts about my earlier therapy session. I kept running over in my mind thoughts about the feelings of being unacceptable and wondering whether, in the end, even God might say to me "You are not worthy."

A week later, I reported a second dream which occurred as I was waking up two days after last week's session. My journal record of the dream reads:

> *I was in a large space, like a warehouse. Many*
> *people were busy moving about, finishing some*
> *project or another. As we were thinking we were*
> *nearly finished working, the man bossing the work*
> *began telling us to take off our clothes, down to our*
> *underwear. I suddenly had the feeling, the realization*
> *in this dream, that the boss meant to do us harm.*
> *I decided to leave the building, escape the danger,*
> *and in the process of leaving, I became aware I was*
> *waking up.*

My recollection of the dream is that it did not involve terror. It was simply a matter of fact that I left the building. It seemed others were leaving too, but I was only focused on my decision to leave. This dream marked an apparent turning in addressing my deeply hidden issues. Again, the words in my journal:

> *Dr. A. felt that it (the dream) was very significant,*
> *that it suggested that my psyche has turned a corner,*
> *and that I will begin to deal with whatever it is in the*
> *distant past that has given me a deep-seated sense that*
> *I'm not good-enough, that I am not wanted.*

Several days later, a third dream was worth recording in my journal. It was calm and carried feelings of being in control of my security.

> *In the dream, I found myself on the second floor*

*of a house that was a lot like my childhood home
in Sandusky. As my wife and I were starting to
prepare for bed, we heard a couple of thumping
sounds in the attic. We thought someone was above
us. I went to the door to the attic at the end of the
hallway. I opened the door and started up the stairs.
I tried to turn on the light, but the bulb must have
been burned out. I called out "Who's there?" No
answer. I called again. "Who's there? Come out,
or I'll call the police." I asked my wife to bring a
flashlight and a baseball bat. She didn't bring them;
maybe she couldn't find them. Finally, I told the
intruder he or she could stay if he or she wanted, but
couldn't escape anyway because I would just hold
the door until the police came.*

I sensed that the dream was a realization that I did not need to be terrified by unknown things. I would be able to find ways to deal with them.

In February of 2012, I was faced with having to go to the hospital for a scan of my lungs because of a concern for what appeared to be an unexplained spot which showed up on an X-ray. There was concern that something had not cleared up after treatment for a bronchial infection. When I reported this upcoming visit to Dr. A, she wondered what feelings I had about having to face a medical issue. I replied that it made me "disgusted," and "I'm not supposed to be not well."

Dr. A. noted that the word "disgusted" is a judgmental word. "It's a word connected to the way in which you are critical and unaccepting of yourself." She observed that "the person inside you needs love and care." Those words struck close. I actually blurted out: *"Watch out! You're hitting close."* The words came on an impulse, without thinking. Painful feelings were starting to rise. I could feel it in my throat. Her words "the person inside you needs love and care" triggered again the pain and the sadness. A minute or two of quiet weeping followed. A softly murmured question, spoken from puzzlement, came up: *"How could I learn to provide love and care to the person inside – the pained little boy who still needs to feel wanted and secure?"*

Our work began to deal with feelings I knew as a kid when Mom wasn't available to me. Dr. A. asked again about not being able to hug my Mom. It was because her face continued to tingle for a long time after she came home. The pain was so great she could not bear to be touched. Because I could not touch her or be close, I would turn to my Dad.

This led Dr. A. to ask me to explore feelings in a role play. I was to imagine myself as a child telling Mom what it felt like not to be able to touch or hug her because her face tingled so much – what it felt like not to have her available to me. As I write this, the feelings and the essence of the words come up again.

> Mom, it's really hard not to be able to hug you or to touch you because your face hurts. Sometimes, you seem like you don't want me near you and that hurts. And then I have to ask Daddy to help me. But what I want is a hug.

And then the role play was directed to my Dad.

> Daddy, I like it when you help me with stuff. You're busy a lot, but you take me places sometimes and help me when you can. I wish Mom would get better. I want her to hug me.

This reliving of the feelings from long ago was extremely painful and tearful and one of the most physically tiring elements of this process. It took a few moments to return slowly to the present. Dr. A. stressed that it is important for me to nurture and love the little boy who was hurt so long ago. I have been judging him as unworthy for a long time.

Near the end of the session I said I was finding it difficult to work my way through the book Dr. A. had recommended: *The Mindful Way though Depression: Freeing Yourself from Chronic Unhappiness.* I was able to read only a small part of it at any one time. Later in the month, I started attending an eight-session workshop taught by Dr. A., based on the book.

I began to grasp its contents and learn to do the recommended meditative practices.

Our session in March started with my reporting on the continued effort to overcome the infection that had been in my lung. When asked about my response to having a challenging health issue, I admitted that it produced some anxiety about whether I would ever get well. And at one point, thinking about it at night, I recalled the experience of having my tonsils out as a young child. Although I'm not clear about what age this might have happened, I recalled waking and standing in a crib in the hospital. I recall the crib's high sides and spaced metal rods…the room being dim…being very unhappy and wanting to go home. I remember Daddy being there for me. My little-boy word "Daddy" crept into my recollection. I remember his promising to get me ice cream on the way home. If Mom was there, I don't recall her. Dr. A. urged me to try to recall other feelings, particularly about my Dad.

I chose to describe experiencing the end of Dad's life. As the pain of his loss began to rise in my chest, I suddenly realized that the anniversary of his death had gone by ten days earlier on March 6. It took a moment to recall the year: 1990, twenty-two years earlier. The day had gone by without my remembering it. Dr. A. asked me what I recalled of my Dad's dying. It's hard, even now, for me to re-type the narrative of his last days. The lump in the throat and the tears are here again. He meant so much to me through the years when I couldn't feel warmth from Mom. Not long after his death I wrote in my journal.

> On Sunday, March 4, after church, we visited Dad
> at the nursing home in Pleasant Hill. He was aware,
> but very weak. While we were there, a minister
> friend of the family from Atlanta arrived. He could
> see that Dad had little strength. After a short visit
> and a brief prayer, Roger left to drive back to Atlanta.
> Ginny and I stayed a while longer, but we both
> needed to head back to Chattanooga in order to go to
> work on Monday.
>
> Writing about it now, I don't know why we didn't

*feel we should tell our employers we needed to stay
by Dad's bedside. I don't know why we didn't make
more of an effort to get a realistic assessment of how
much longer Dad might live. But we didn't. I have
a lingering sense that he really wanted us to leave
and not miss our job responsibilities. I also sense that
being in the presence of my dying parent was a reality
I didn't want to face. That reality allowed us to drive
the eighty miles home to Chattanooga.*

*Tuesday evening, Dad died. Later, we learned he had
urged Mom to have some supper with a very close
family friend. Not long after arriving there, she got
a call asking her to return to the nursing home. Dad
died before she got back. We have often thought that
he wanted the end to come this way. Perhaps he tried
to protect her from being overwhelmed by emotion, as
he often did. My brother asked the funeral director
to defer the cremation until we could arrive for a last
goodbye. We were ushered into a side room. Dad
was lying on a gurney, wrapped in a red blanket.
Only his face was visible. I could barely look at his
face as the tears flooded to my eyes, the grief was
so terribly intense. The father with whom I had
consulted so often about things of interest to us both
could no longer speak to me, nor I to him. Mercifully,
for him, the pain of illness was over. For me, the pain
had only begun.*

Now, responding to Dr. A.'s question, the grief was flooding back. I began to talk about the good things Daddy did with me. He built a swing and seesaw in our back yard in Bridgeport. He had a workbench in the basement and a modest collection of tools. Mostly, I watched him work on making the parts: the braces for the posts and the crossbar for the swing, and the side brace for the see-saw built to the left of the swing. I helped him paint them. That was the project that gave me my first rudimentary lessons in woodworking. These were skills I honed and expanded years later in my own home.

I have never forgotten the day Dad took me back to the circus to get another balloon to replace the first one I got when "Keever," Mrs. McKeever, the secretary at the church, took me to the circus earlier that day. It was her way of giving me a caring gift in the middle of Mom's illness. When I got home, I accidently let go of the balloon and watched helplessly as it floated away into the blue sky. I was absolutely heart-broken and inconsolable. I hounded Daddy until he relented and took me back to get another one. That one I tied to my bunk bed, and it hung there until long after the helium leaked out. I know now that that first balloon took on great significance because it became what psychologists call a transitional love object. It represented the attention I received from "Keever." My attachment was moving from my mother to another person who offered care and safety in Mom's absence.

Continuing the role play, I turned away from Dr. A. and began to talk to my Dad as if he were sitting in the empty wing chair to my right. I thanked him for being such a caregiver to me. I was realizing how hard it must have been for him to be the caregiver that Mom was not able to be because she became so dependent on him after her illness. As I talked, it began to dawn on me what a high price he paid, in terms of the burdens he carried, in order to sustain our family and hold it together. The realization both saddens me and makes me grateful for what he struggled to do and for what he accomplished in the effort to create memorable experiences for us as a family.

Probably the greatest experiences were the two trips we took as a family by car, first to the west coast in 1952, and later to Colorado and Wyoming in 1954. They both involved camping, but the first trip was epic. Imagine a family of six, Mom and Dad and four boys, travelling in an un-airconditioned Ford sedan, across the United States. Our parents were delegates to a national meeting in Pomona, California. We drove for a week, crossing the Midwest, following as much of the Oregon Trail as possible, past Chimney Rock and Scotts Bluff in Nebraska, on to Fort Bridger and Laramie, Wyoming and through the Wasatch Mountains, across the great

Salt Lake Desert and over Donner Pass, into California arriving at Mom's sister's home in Palo Alto. We boys stayed there while the folks went on to Pomona, and a week later we made side trips in California. The trip back took the southern route to see the Bryce and Zion Canyons, the Grand Canyon, the Petrified Forest and the Painted Desert, before turning east and heading home to Ohio. I'm still in awe of that achievement and am grateful for learning so much about our country and history.

In an early April session, I was again struggling with my continuing regret, sadness and guilt about the pain I have caused my sons through my divorce, an event now more than twenty-six years in the past. These feelings have caused moments of not believing I am worthy of love from my sons or my present wife. Dr. A. encouraged me to make a specific trip to visit my younger son and his wife, to share with them my regret for the pain I have caused and to again apologize to them. I did so. Our time together was painful, honest and deeply loving. Earlier visits with my older son and his wife have brought resolution and closer connection for us as well.

The second session in April dealt first with the helpful and meaningful outcomes from my visit with my son and his wife. Then Dr. A. asked me to describe my perceptions and feelings about my marriage during the two years in my first church. These were the years when the boys were born. The first son came in September 1963, a month after I began serving the little country church. The second was born at the beginning of March 1965. Over those seventeen months, I began to feel that the babies had more of my wife's attention than I did. In reality, that was a necessity because the boys were infants. Even so, as the years passed, similar feelings continued. As the result of my therapy, I know that those feelings were deeply connected to the loss of warmth from my mother at the time of her illness and afterward. But from the birth of the boys and beyond, I was only able to feel the resurfacing of old feelings. I had no idea of their source and came to feel I was stuck in a lonely situation that would not ever change.

Having been introduced to wine and alcoholic drinks during my internship three years earlier, the use of alcohol at night and on weekends

became a too-frequent avenue for attempting to feel better. I now
know that the drinking was an attempt not only to sooth the feelings of
discouragement, but also a manifestation of unrecognized depression.

My journal entry for the therapy session of April 27, 2012 concludes
with these words: *The pain of the memories made the tears flow. I now feel
someone has finally heard my real feelings from that long-ago time. I know that the
tears were connected to the trauma of my childhood. I know I still have more work
to do.*

A Time for Joy and Sadness: 2012-2013

After the April sessions, I stopped therapy to focus on other
activities. In June Ginny and I were working on repainting bedrooms.
Then, suddenly in mid-July, Ginny's elderly, great aunt Mary entered
her last illness. We flew to St. Paul, Minnesota to visit her on the last
day she had any real strength. We saw her the next morning before
having to leave. She was essentially unresponsive. Before leaving, I
bent close to her and offered a brief prayer and blessing. We managed
to hold our emotions in check until we were in the hallway, and then
the tears overwhelmed us. A chaplain invited us to sit with her for a
few moments in a small meditation room before going to the car.

Aunt Mary held on for six more days. The memorial service was
arranged for mid-August. We drove back to Minnesota where I conducted a
private graveside memorial service and the interment of her ashes on August
18. After two days helping with the task of sorting and moving the items
from the now-vacant apartment, we drove home to Virginia.

A Last Reunion

Six weeks later, in October, we drove to Murphy in western North
Carolina for a visit with my brothers Alan and Frank and their wives, Kittie
and Kathy. Alan and his wife retired to Murphy more than a decade earlier.
Frank and Kathy came east from Eugene, Oregon to be with us, as he
explained: "because I wanted to see the fall colors in the hardwood forests
one more time." He had aged a great deal over the half dozen years since

he last visited us. He had lost weight and was no longer the robust person I remembered. He was on dialysis for several years and was aware at age seventy-two, though he mentioned it only once, that he probably did not have many more years.

Our time together was a wonderful reconnecting. I shared much of what I knew about my traumatic experience with our Mom's illness when Greg was born. We reminisced about him, and our mixed feelings of sadness and pain that he died at such a young age, fifty-seven, a victim of addiction. These were the most meaningful and intimate few days we three brothers and our wives ever spent together.

During this visit, I shared news of my upcoming assignment beginning in November. I had accepted an invitation to serve as the interim pastor of Immanuel United Church of Christ at Cambridge on Maryland's Eastern Shore. I knew many in this congregation because I was the consultant and campaign director several years earlier when the congregation raised sufficient funds to build its new church. The area leader of our denomination included my name on the list of candidates for the interim position. This was for me a significant reaffirmation of my pastoral calling. I was honored by the confidence the congregation placed in me.

My agreement committed me to serve the balance of the interim period between pastors until a new full-time pastor was called by the congregation. To fulfill the agreement, I drove the one hundred miles from home to the Eastern Shore on Wednesday or Thursday, depending on which evening I had a committee meeting. I lived in the church's parsonage, stayed through my Sunday obligations and returned home later on Sunday afternoon. I was thankful for the opportunity to serve again in the role of pastor and teacher, to conduct the sacraments of communion and baptism, and to lead worship. During those five and half months, I conducted three funerals. They were planned and led with more sensitivity and consideration than was the case with the very first funeral I conducted that gray, dismal day at Glenville Congregational Church in Cleveland during my internship fifty-one years earlier. This was the second spiritually fulfilling parish assignment since my "retirement" in 2000.

2013: ILLNESS AND LOSS

In February, while still involved at Immanuel, I scheduled a session with Dr. A. Its primary focus was a review of how I was responding to the work with the church in Cambridge. Overall, I felt positive about it and happy that I had taken on the task. In the end, the church was able to call its permanent pastor and arrange a starting date in mid-April, when duties ended.

Just over a month after I finished in Cambridge, Alan called to tell me he was in the hospital in Atlanta and facing major surgery. He complained of feeling pains after playing golf. His doctor sent him to a cardiologist who referred him to a medical center in Atlanta for an angioplasty to open one blockage. However, the doctors discovered multiple blockages and immediately scheduled open-heart surgery for two days later on May 22, Alan's seventy-first birthday. The surgeons were amazed that he had not had a major heart attack. Even so, he came through surgery and proceeded to recover well, religiously doing his heart rehabilitation exercises.

A month and a day after Alan's surgery, he called around noon on a Sunday. This time, he relayed sad news. My brother Frank's wife, Kathy, had called from Eugene, Oregon to say Frank was in the hospital, and that he was not likely to live through the day. I was crushed. There was no point in anyone trying to get to Eugene to see him. Later that evening, June 24, Kathy called with word that Frank died about 3:00 p.m., Eastern time. He had developed a blood clot very high in his left leg. It was inoperable, and he could not survive. Kathy said that the woman physician who spoke with her about Frank's condition and prognosis was very kind and very helpful, explaining that Frank's leg had been without oxygen too long. This, and his vascular difficulties from years of dialysis, made surgery impossible. She assured Kathy that Frank was comfortable, and likely felt no pain. Kathy told me she recognized that it was necessary to let Frank go.

There were lots of tears on the phone. Once more, overwhelming sadness filled my chest and heart. Now I had only one living brother. He, too, faced health challenges, still recovering from open heart surgery. Kathy said she didn't want us to come to Eugene. We should wait until later in the summer or early fall when we could plan a memorial service, and Alan would be recovered sufficiently to be able to fly to Oregon.

At the end of June, Ginny and I flew to Long Beach, California for the biennial gathering of the national body of the United Church of Christ. Ginny was an official delegate and I was free to enjoy whatever sessions interested me. Following the meeting, we enjoyed a two-day visit in San Diego with Tom Ryan, and his wife. Tom was one of my two best friends in high school. With the exception of our fiftieth high school reunion, I had not seen him since our sophomore year when he and his family moved to California.

The balance of August involved continuing to paint bedrooms and having the floors refinished. We watched landscapers transform our yard, as we began to anticipate preparations for the day when we would decide to give up our four-bedrooms, split-level house and too-big yard. During these months, I also continued to be involved with the planning committee for my fiftieth reunion at Yale Divinity School. I served as chair of the committee raising funds for the Class of 1963's endowed scholarship. The highlight was to be the presentation of a ceremonial check to Dean Sterling during the reunion luncheon.

In two sessions over July and August, Dr. A. and I continued to deal with my grief over the loss of Frank and Alan's health challenges. I felt disconnected from my inner self. Impatient with the continuing feelings of loss, I wondered "What's wrong with me?" Once again, the self-criticism reared up. Dr. A. reminded me of the need to develop compassion for myself and for the presence of the pain. She was suggesting a way to "welcome" the hurt in the context of simply recognizing that the pain of grief is present, and thus not judge or criticize myself for experiencing it again. She was reminding me of skills from the practice of mindfulness.

Meanwhile, during the summer, Frank's wife arranged his

memorial service. It was held early in October in the chapel of the First Congregational Church (UCC) of Eugene, attended by family and close friends. She asked me to conduct the service, which I did. This was difficult, and at one point I had to pause during my tribute to his life to regain my composure. Alan read the Scripture passages chosen for the day. In spite of deep sadness, the service was a very meaningful time for us all, mixed with humorous stories and meditative reflection.

Kathy and Frank met while they were students at Union Theological Seminary in New York City. They were still in contact with a significant number of their closest friends from those years, and several of them came to Eugene for the service. Two of them came from Atlanta, and one of them paid for a seat on the plane for his cello. He played it during the service, a very moving tribute to his friend and former seminary classmate. Another friend came from Hawaii and lifted our spirits with humorous tales about the ways in which Frank helped him study for final exams.

Following the service, on a gorgeous October day, we drove up into the Cascade Range to McKenzie Pass. Our destination was a vast ancient expanse of black volcanic rock, an area Frank loved. We scattered some of his ashes there. It seemed a timeless place, one that reminded us of the same timelessness he studied as a scholar of the Psalms and ancient Hebrew Scriptures.

Two days after we arrived home, we drove to New Haven to attend the annual Convocation and fiftieth reunion of my class at Yale Divinity School. Our goal was to achieve a minimum of fifty-thousand dollars in pledged commitments with which to establish the Class of 1963 Scholarship. We were pleased to present a gift in excess of sixty-two thousand dollars to Dean Sterling. Our class achieving its highest reunion attendance ever was an added pleasure.

THE INNER CRITIC

From August through the end of the year, my therapy sessions continued to focus on my experiences of grieving and my inner critic which was asking negative questions: "What's wrong with me?" "Why was my career such a mishmash?" "Why is it that I could not stay in a job more than a few years?" "How was it my Dad could serve two long pastorates, one of thirteen years and another of eleven, and a decade-long appointment in our church's national offices, and I could only achieve short tenures?"

Added to this was a continuing self-judgment about having ended my first marriage. This still lingered, even though I had feedback pointing to factors which worked against the possibility of a successful marriage. There were feelings of shame and a sense of failure which remained unresolved. Healing would take more time.

A third dynamic was at work which was only beginning to come into focus. The inner critic sometimes asked the question: "Why would anybody want to love me?" In another form, the question emerged in several questions to my wife. One version was "What did you ever see in me?" Or it would come out sideways in the statement "You really *do* love me," as if there had been some doubt about it. This was a hurtful manifestation of the inner critic, because it caused Ginny to feel that I had doubts about her commitment. It did not help matters when I would try to say I meant the remark as a compliment. She heard it to mean I had some doubt. Ginny would reflect the feelings in her reply: "You mean there is some question about whether I love you?" As I was to learn later, this sort of back and forth was born out of the anxious attachment with Mom which resulted from the aftermath of her illness. Now it was being carried forward into my marriage.

In the last weeks of 2013, along with these issues, I continued to struggle with the realization that I now had only one living brother. In addition, I began to feel the anticipatory grief connected to the likelihood that I would be the sole survivor of a family of six. My two sons and their three children, along with Alan's son, would be the only legacies remaining after I am gone.

NEW REALIZATIONS AND FINAL LOSSES

In the first two months of 2014, our work focused on learning to trust

Ginny's love for me, and to identify the sources of my tendency to express, in off-handed ways, disbelief that anyone would really want to love me. In a guided dialogue in which I imagined the words Ginny might use to assure me of her commitment and love for me, I began to realize how my uncertainties came across to her. In succeeding months, this lingering anxiety from the past faded away.

In April 2014, I underwent major surgery for a reverse shoulder replacement. This was made necessary as the result of two falls suffered in our yard the previous summer. They tore the rotator cuff in my right shoulder so severely it could not be repaired. A long process of rehabilitation restored full use of my arm. The same spring and early summer provided me the opportunity to participate in Dr. A.'s eight two-hour sessions of mindfulness education.

More illness

In the summer, my brother Alan called to tell me that he had suffered another setback. He was diagnosed with idiopathic pulmonary fibrosis, a deterioration of lung tissue which ultimately would be fatal. The doctors could not say how long he might live. There was a medication which, with the help of supplemental oxygen at night, would slow the progress of the disease. This was a stunning blow after having survived quintuple heart bypass surgery a little more than a year earlier.

However, he was strong enough to come to Washington from North Carolina to join me in attending the funeral for Captain Bill H., U.S. Army (ret.), the husband of our cousin, Sue. She and her family came from Oregon for the service and burial with full military honors at Arlington National Cemetery. Her three sisters and their families were also present. The ceremonies were held on July 30, 2014. It was a beautiful summer morning. Alan and I walked the full distance behind the caisson with other mourners as we proceeded across Arlington National Cemetery from the Old Post Chapel at Fort Meyer to the Columbarium for the placement of Bill's ashes. After the service, I wrote about the sights and sounds of that solemn day to share with Sue. With her permission, the narrative is included here.

Honoring Capt. William H... (USA, ret.) at Arlington National Cemetery

William H. was a world-renowned surgeon. A pioneer in developing the auditory brain stem implant, he performed more than 6,000 surgeries to remove brain tumors known as acoustic neuromas. Some of the doctors who studied under him came across the country to attend the services.

Wednesday, July 30, 2014, was a crystal clear, bright sunny morning as family and friends gathered in the parking lot facing the tall spire of the Old Post Chapel at Fort Myer in Arlington, Virginia. The chapel is reminiscent of a classic, New England brick meeting house with its tall white steeple and simple classic lines. People stood in clusters, talking with one another in quiet tones. I was trying to place the correct names with the faces of people Alan and I and our wives met the previous evening at the family dinner.

While waiting to enter the chapel, Sue was quietly greeting mourners. She is a tall, elegant and strikingly attractive woman. She wore a simple black dress, her blond hair tied neatly in a bun. The easy and light-hearted banter of the previous evening's dinner gathering was gone. Now, she moved among family and close friends with a quiet, assured manner that masked what must have been a deepening sense of the finality the day's events would bring. Five months had passed between Bill's death and this day. A large piece of the grieving had been postponed. In these moments, its reality was rising again. And the hurt and loss began to etch somberness on her face. It would deepen over the morning.

In the course of the next few moments, two contingents of honor guards began assembling, along with a military band. A few minutes before nine, the mourners were directed to the chapel. At the conclusion of the organ prelude, the chapel doors were closed, and two members of the honor guard stepped with slow precision to the front of the chapel. One carried the polished wooden box containing Bill's ashes, and the other an American flag folded in a triangle. These were placed on a small table at the foot of the steps to the altar.

The service was brief. It included prayers and Scripture readings by a military chaplain. Ann, my cousin Sue's daughter, read a warm and heartfelt remembrance of her stepfather, a caring and generous man who supported her through medical school. She returned to the front row, sitting next to her mother with other family members, including Sue's three sisters. At the conclusion of the singing of a hymn, the honor guard, with great precision and formality, retrieved the simple wooden box and flag, and making an about face in unison, proceeded with measured paces back up the aisle, the family and guests processing respectfully behind.

THE PROCESSION

As we stepped back into the sunshine, the scene had changed. Now the caisson and its team of six white horses had been drawn up. Two riders were up on the lead horses, sitting ramrod straight in their dress blue army uniforms. The two honor bearers placed the urn in a special compartment in the casket atop the caisson. Mourners who wished to walk to the columbarium behind the caisson were directed to their positions. Those who wanted to drive were to fall in behind the walkers. My brother Alan and I walked to honor Sue's husband, a man we had met only twice at family events to celebrate Sue's mother's 90th and 95th birthdays.

At the order of the drum major, the drummers began the marching cadences. They quickly brought me back to my days in high school and college marching bands. The hair on the back of my neck began to stand. As we started off, my left foot stepped to the first beat of the cadence, the first move taught to every band member. Even though the sound grew distant as the flag bearers and band leading the procession and moved ahead of the horse-drawn caisson, the muffled cadence stayed with me. Ta-rum, ta-rum, ta-rum, rum, rum; Ta-rum, ta-rum, ta-rum, rum, rum. On it went, over and over, the steady drumbeat of the marching cadence. The emotion of it as I write the words still causes my eyes to well up. As a tribute to honor

Bill and support Sue and her family, walking to the cadence was the least Alan and I could do to feel as if we had paid tribute in some small way.

From time to time, the band played military music or a Sousa march, but the cadence never stopped. Through groves of trees, down sloping pathways, up winding, shaded hills we went, passing old grave markers and monuments from the earliest days of the cemetery. There were headstones and oversized monuments marking the resting places of service people from the Civil War onward, to the wars of the 20th century and the more recent gleaming white rows of simple headstones marking those who gave what Lincoln called "their last full measure of devotion" in the arid landscapes of Iraq and Afghanistan.

On that sunny July morning, under a deep blue sky, the sound of the military band wafted back to us on the warming air. And always, between the playing of the marches, the steady cadence went on, like a never-failing heartbeat: Ta-rum, Ta-rum, Ta-rum, rum, rum; until we had walked the full mile across Arlington National Cemetery to the Columbarium, a stone structure containing rows of niches, each designed to receive an urn containing the ashes of a fallen member of the military. Bill's ashes were interred there, and a plate on the closed niche recoded the particulars: his name, rank, branch, and dates of service.

The most somber moment came when Sue and her sisters were seated beneath a canopied gathering area adjacent to the Columbarium. Following the brief service by the chaplain and presentation of the folded flag to Sue, one of the women who volunteers at Arlington Cemetery, escorted by a military officer, stepped forward and knelt in front of Sue to express condolences and offer assistance. It was a deeply touching moment of private expression in a very public place.

Bill was a hero, not just because he served, but because after his service, he performed many, many surgeries, at no charge, on wounded soldiers who suffered from illnesses of the auditory system. This dedicated surgeon restored hearing and healed cancers as his gift to America's service men and women. And now his remains are together with those who served their country, and whom he served, a bond unbroken for all time. May God grant him peace.

~

For the balance of 2014, therapy sessions were intermittent. I was increasingly involved with volunteer responsibilities at church, among them leading the annual campaign for financial support, beginning the preparation of a six-session class for adult learners about Christian mysticism and stories of some of the great mystics. In the fall, I agreed to be nominated to become the Moderator-elect for 2015, and then Moderator, the top volunteer leader in our congregation. In effect, I would be an understudy during 2015, and then chair the governing body called the Church Council for 2016. The election was to take place on the last Sunday of January in 2015.

UNPLANNED HOSPITAL STAY

Unfortunately, January 2015 brought unexpected health challenges. I first began to feel unwell on Tuesday, the sixth. It didn't act like flu, but I was feeling weak and coughing a lot. By afternoon, I was holding on, knowing that I had a pre-arranged appointment with the doctor on Thursday morning. The doctor decided I was suffering from asthma and gave me a prescription for an antibiotic and an inhaler.

I went home and began ten days of taking a daily 500-milligram antibiotic. I slept for most of the next two days and began to feel better, but could not attend church on Sunday, the 11th. By the end of the antibiotics on the following Saturday, I felt much better, but still had an occasional cough. I went to church on Sunday, the 18th.

The following Thursday evening, I began to feel a mild soreness in my right chest. The next day it seemed to be getting worse. The pain was more noticeable and beginning to be worrisome. On Saturday, the 24th, by mid-afternoon, the pain was bad enough to frighten me with the thought that something was seriously wrong. Shortly before 4:00 p.m., struggling to breathe without causing sharp pain, Ginny took me to the Emergency Room at Mt. Vernon Hospital, a mere ten minutes from home.

Arriving at the reception desk at the Emergency Room, I told the receptionist I was having real pain in my right chest, about seven on a scale of zero to ten. She took some brief information and then found my records of previous visits in her computer. She placed a printed ID band on my right wrist. Within five minutes of sitting down in the waiting area, an aide arrived and ushered me into the first treatment bay, took a quick electrocardiogram, and then wheeled me to a bed in alcove fourteen of the ER.

The testing began immediately: vital signs, pulse, temperature and blood pressure. The little clamp that clips onto a finger was applied to measure oxygen level in the blood stream, an amazing device. A heart monitor was connected, and blood drawn. An oxygen tube was affixed beneath my nose to assist my breathing. An intravenous (IV) tube was connected and a saline drip started. A second EKG was run. Soon, a portable x-ray machine arrived, and a picture of my chest was made. After about forty-five minutes the level of activity subsided, but a nurse would periodically check readings on the monitor. Later, after it was found that my issue was an infection in my right lung, antibiotic drugs were added to the IV.

By now, the realization that skilled people were caring for me, combined with the supplemental oxygen and resting in the ER with Ginny close by, my anxiety and the pain in my chest began to ease. I was grateful to be in the care of skilled people who could find the source of my pain, and, hopefully, overcome the cause of my illness.

A while later, an attending doctor announced that I would be staying in the hospital, and that they would "send me upstairs" when a bed became available. By now it was nearly 7:00 pm. Someone asked if I was hungry. The answer was "yes," and some food was ordered for me and another patient in a nearby alcove. Ginny went to find the cafeteria which was near closing. She returned, having changed her mind about finding food.

Now time dragged. It seemed nothing was happening. I was lying on an ER gurney, my upper body clothed in a hospital gown and a light blanket spread over me. There was an odd dissonance to the fact that I was still dressed in half of my street clothes, my tan pants and brown shoes protruding at the foot of the blanket. Eventually an aide came, hooked me to a portable monitor and wheeled me in a chair to the elevators, to the sixth floor, the telemetry unit, room 632, bed B, the one by the window. It was now nearly 8:30 p.m.

The portable monitor was detached. I took off my shoes, socks, and remaining clothes. Now, I was clad solely in a hospital gown, one of the show-it-all types, which Ginny kindly tied in the back. The nurse attached more, and different, tabs to the skin of my chest to connect the wires of a portable telemetry monitor. She placed the small, square battery-driven transmitter in the right breast pocket of the gown. I settled into the bed that would be home for what turned out to be the next thirty-six hours.

The nurse left. Ginny, looking very tired, sat in the chair nearby. Now that the crisis was controlled, it seemed we were taking a few minutes to absorb this new reality. I suggested that Ginny go home. She agreed and leaned over for a goodnight kiss. Quietly, she stepped around the curtain and was gone.

Not long after, Dr. John S. came in. He was the on-call house physician for the weekend. He confirmed that I was suffering from pneumonia. I knew who he was, and so I expressed my condolences to him on the recent death of his father, who had owned a restaurant Ginny and I patronized. Dr. S. sat on the edge of my bed. We had what amounted to a pastoral conversation about the process of grieving the loss of one's father. It was a conversation that took place as if we were old friends. Turning to me, he let me know he had ordered a CT scan just to be sure there wasn't some hidden problem in my lungs. He also told me he had asked a pulmonologist to stop by in the morning.

One more interruption intruded before I was left to the night routine of the telemetry unit. About 10:00 p.m., an aide arrived with a wheelchair and announced that she was taking me down to the radiology unit for the CT scan. By the time we arrived, I was shivering in my scant hospital gown. With the scan completed, I was bundled back into my wheelchair, wrapped in a warm blanket, which ended the shivers, and wheeled back to my bed by the window in room 632.

I stood by the window, taking a moment to be distracted from the reality of the moment. Outside, night had descended. From the sixth floor of the hospital, the nearly- deserted visitors parking lot was spread below. Now, it looked lonely in the night light, its evenly marked parking spaces abandoned until the day-time business of healthcare resumed its hurried pace. In the distance, the homes and townhouses of the neighborhood were visible in the soft glow of distant streetlamps. The bright red traffic lights on Sherwood Hall Lane, periodically changing to green, marked the intersections. Occasionally, a vehicle glided through the scene on the street beyond the expansive roof of the Mt. Vernon Government Center. In the quiet of the night, a neighborhood I knew very well was a world beyond my reach. I got into bed.

Now, my world was governed by the rhythms of the hospital and its staff. They had control of my life. I pulled the cord to the overhead light. It switched to high, briefly startling me. I pulled it again, and the light went out. I closed my eyes, grateful to be breathing with virtually no pain. There would be little sleep this night or the next. In the nurses' station beyond the door, someone was listening for the sound of any alarm on the telemetry unit that would alert nurses that I or another patient was facing some sort of heart episode. The thought that I was one of the monitored patients produced some anxiety, until I decided that this was a safety precaution, not an omen of a life-threatening condition.

The next day, Sunday, was uneventful. I missed the annual meeting of our church but was elected Moderator-elect in my absence. I was released on Monday morning, tired but grateful. And feeling no pain. I vowed to myself that I would guard against letting any future infections get a serious grip. For the first time, I was frightened by an awareness of the threat of death. This was a fright I don't want to repeat, not for a good number of years.

A Grand Trip

In September 2015, Ginny and I embarked on a driving trip to Oregon to visit Kathy, Frank's widow. We drove to Minnesota to visit family over Labor Day weekend, and then started west through Iowa and South Dakota to Rapid City, and then to Cody, Wyoming and a wonderful exhibit of western art in the Buffalo Bill Cody Museum. Our visit to Yellowstone National Park and the Old Faithful geyser was a first for Ginny. The rest of the trip included historic places along the Oregon Trail in Idaho. The last leg included turning north in Idaho to enjoy a morning trip through the Columbia River Gorge to Portland and then south to Eugene.

We had a truly enjoyable re-connecting with cousin Sue and Frank's Kathy. On the return trip, we saw more of the West, crossing the high desert of Oregon east of Bend to Boise and then south in Utah to turn east at Salt Lake City. The last legs of the trip included visits to Fort Bridger, Laramie, Wyoming and the art museum at the University of Wyoming. After an overnight, we drive south to visit Big Thompson Canyon and Estes, Colorado at the edge of Rocky Mountain National Park. An overnight in Boulder afforded us a visit with Ginny's niece before we started the long trip back to Virginia.

We arrived home safely after a trip of twenty-four days and seven thousand miles. However, six days later, Ginny fell from the second stairstep home and broke her ankle in three places. I became nursemaid for six weeks while she was required to stay off her feet. She was liberated to crutches a few days before Christmas. Soon after she switched to a walker and slowly regained mobility over the next several weeks.

Stresses and Loss Again

The stresses continued in 2016. What therapy sessions I did schedule dealt with difficulties and emotions arising from a challenging personnel issue I had to address in my volunteer role at church. Caring for Ginny and working through her recuperation from two more surgeries to cure infections in her repaired ankle also took my energy and attention.

In April, we drove to Murphy, North Carolina to visit Alan and his wife. Frank's widow came from Oregon and the five of us had a wonderful time. Alan was still swinging a golf club, and I vowed I would come back in June to play nine holes with him.

It was not to be. I didn't get there in June and Alan died suddenly on July 1. Once again, the pain of grief descended. During the memorial service on July 7, led by their minister, I offered a remembrance of Alan. Now I was the lone survivor of the four "Petey Boys," as we had been affectionately known when we were kids in Sandusky.

To make matters worse, my good friend, the Rev. Dr. John Deckenback, the Conference Minister (the executive leader) of our church's regional judicatory, unexpectedly died at his desk on July 19. I worked with John for more than a decade as chair of the new church development committee. A year earlier he recognized my work at the annual meeting of the Conference. His sudden death was a terrible blow, not only to his family, but also to a great many people who had worked with him over more than two decades. Once again, I was experiencing deep grief and loss, and again, Dr. A. helped me walk through the inevitable pain. To find rest and restoration, Ginny and I spent two weeks at the beach at the end of August and into early September, just being away from all that had happened.

Two sessions with Dr. A. in that autumn dealt with a sudden recurrence of my emotions about my Mom and re-opened the efforts to heal the pained and lost little boy.

Chapter 11

Awaking to Awareness:

Healing the Lost Boy

I N ORDER TO UNCOVER AND DEAL WITH THE AFTERMATH OF MY LONG-SUPPRESSED TRAUMA, DR. A. continued to stress the importance of being kind and caring of my inner little boy. Her encouragement brought to mind a short period of counseling I experienced many years earlier. I found notes in an older journal about several sessions in 1991. The therapist at the time had directed me to a technique described by psychologist and self-help author John Eliot Bradshaw, who wrote extensively about rediscovering one's inner child. (1)

Responding to the suggestion, I began to work with an exercise which involved writing dialogues between my adult self and my inner little boy. These came to be messages between "Big Rob" and "Little Rob." The essence of these written exchanges was a willingness, albeit tentative, for the two personas to try to get to know one another and understand one another's feelings.

The suggested technique was to write as my current self, using the dominant hand, my left. When the inner child responded, the non-dominant hand would write, my right. The dominant hand naturally wrote in cursive, the non-dominant hand printed. The early efforts at this dialog surfaced some intense feelings of distrust, but a willingness in each to listen to the other. The following are samples from this dialogue. The inner child's responses are in italics.

From mid May 1991:

Dear Little Rob,

I'm glad you were born. I think it's neat you are a baby boy. I like you, and I love you a lot. I want to help you grow up. I want to be there for you. I want to laugh and play and be with you and share the hard times too. Love, Rob

Dear Big Rob, I trust you. I want you to be my friend. I'm afraid. Will you hold my hand?

Love, Little Rob

From early June 1991:

Dear Little Rob,

I'm beginning to not be afraid to meet you. I hope you like the name "Little Rob." It feels Ok to me; does it feel OK to you? Next week with [therapist's] help we'll get to know each other some more. I love you and I think you are a very special little boy.

Love, Big Rob

Dear Big Rob,

I'm glad we're going to get to know each other. I've been waiting a long time. I like the name Little Rob. Robin is a bird. Tweet, tweet! I love you too, Big Rob.

Your friend, Little Rob

In the next session in 1991, the therapist led me on a guided fantasy to my infancy and first home. The exercise was to imagine myself holding me as an infant. I spoke the lines above first as my present-day self and then as myself as an infant speaking to my adult self. Each persona surfaced feelings of not being certain we could trust the other.

A week after this exercise, we spent a significant amount of time exploring feelings and relating them to learnings from earlier sessions. Important realizations emerged. My notes read:

> *Though I feel that somewhere, very early on, I was*
> *truly loved and held by my mother, I also feel that*
> *somewhere early in my life she let go of me. I learned*
> *not to trust or to believe that anyone really cared for*
> *me. And I developed an enormous need for approval.*

Suddenly, as I read this again, I realized that this was written as a response in my head, not with any connection to the feelings underneath it.

The therapy sessions in 1991 were interrupted by family events. My older son was married in the last week of June. We were on a two-week vacation to Vermont in the first half of July. In August, my mother, who was eighty-four years old, fell and broke her hip at her retirement home in Tennessee. This required a trip from Fredericksburg, Virginia.

There is a brief note following what probably was a session in late September in which I refer to feeling "tethered" to my father and needing to break free. The same note refers to "making a pact before this work is over to find a way to pay tribute to Mom and Dad in spite of the things they didn't do to nurture me." The therapist went on to say she sees good things in them and that "your dad was probably a very pained person inside. He tried so hard to control things, and your mother probably had a great deal of pain as well. They found ways to surmount their pains, fears and limitations." This note suggests to me that I told the therapist in 1991 about my mother's illness and hospitalization, but we never got to the feelings from that time which remained deeply buried.

In early October 1991, a brief note recorded the fact that the therapist's office called and cancelled an appointment because the therapist was ill. Brief and sketchy notes included this comment: "I don't know how much more therapy I can take right now." Thereafter, my life apparently was focused in other directions. There were no further efforts to seek therapy until my inability to function prompted me to reach out to Dr. A. in the summer of 2009. I thought I only required a few sessions to re-start my flagging motivation. Of course, I learned that lack of motivation is one of the significant symptoms of depression.

It is surprising that the therapy in 1991 explored the edges of, but never uncovered, the connection of my issues to the traumatic effect of my mother's illness and her forced absence when I was very young. The profound grief and sadness of the loss never got out. It was Dr. A. who led me to the real source of my depression and deep-seated grief. Much of the work with Dr. A. became the hard work of healing the lost "Little Rob" whom "Big Rob" had begun to try to nurture years earlier.

Now, returning to our work in 2017, Dr. A. and I were focused on both the pain and grief of my childhood experience, and we were dealing with my deep regret about many of the events of my adult life, including the feeling that I had failed in my intended career. These issues also included feelings of being an unworthy person and a nagging wondering about why anybody would want to love me.

The feelings about having a failed career and being unworthy were all connected to the underlying issues of my depression, and recurring periods of feeling "down." The work of healing the lost little boy continued through several sessions, interspersed with several months away from therapy when my attention was directed to other projects and volunteer commitments. However, our work had also given me a number of resources which I used at home to continue the process of recovery.

I returned to working with the book, *The Mindful Way Though Depression*. It provided an introduction to understanding the nature of depression, and a guide to developing a program of mindful awareness to address anxiety and depression. It was a surprise to discover, early on in therapy, I was suffering from depression. When I saw the list of nine indicators (2), I realized that four of them clearly applied to me. I've paraphrased the four as I experienced them.

> a. Low motivation to do what I thought I wanted to do, and was no longer interested in or able to enjoy most of my activities
>
> b. Poor sleep and often napping during the day
>
> c. Frequent tiredness and low energy during the day
>
> d. Feeling less worthy than others; doubted my worth (My "inner critic" was talking!)

Over time, I learned to use mindful awareness to address the symptoms of depression. These techniques began to heal the hurt little boy inside and connect us both so that we were no longer strangers. In addition, I was learning that many of the negative thoughts I experienced from time to time also contributed to negative feelings. Such thoughts were not always present but occurred periodically. I was learning to identify them and begin to defuse them. They included self-critical thoughts like: "I am not good enough," or "I wish I was a better person," or "I am a disappointment to myself."

The strongest, most persistent, of these thoughts has been that I am not a worthy person. Incredible as it sounds, even in the course of my marriage of thirty-two years, the thought continued to occur that it was amazing anyone would want to love me. Each of these thoughts was triggered by the "inner critic" Dr. A. had pointed out to me. We hadn't yet found its source, but I was learning to know its strategies.

A variety of practices have helped me become more mindfully aware. My purpose here is not to provide a primer on how to practice mindfulness. It is to suggest some of the activities which began to change my negative thoughts and feelings, and thus lift the burdensome and depressive "down" feelings which, over many years, accumulated until they became so dispiriting, I had to ask for help.

One of the first practices I learned was a method for paying attention to the various sensations I feel throughout my body. This entailed lying comfortably on a flat surface and taking the time to be aware of the sensations occurring in my body. In following this practice, I learned to recognize the places where I felt tension, discomfort or pain as well as those places which felt comfortable and okay. Each of these sessions began at my toes and continued to the top of my head, taking time to be aware of each part and whatever sensation was there. This became a way of relaxing and accepting, without judging, whatever was occurring in my physical self.

Developing awareness also meant discovering how I contribute to my depression and "down" moods. One of the surest ways was to ruminate about events. When a project did not go well, I would wonder what I had done wrong, or search for what I could have done better. Sometimes, thinking about it, I would chastise myself for not anticipating and preventing an unforeseen contributing factor. Chastising myself is one of the most damaging things I can do to my emotional well-being. Or I might ruminate about the experiences in my life, turning over in my mind the details and the "what-ifs." Such bouts of rumination could go on for long periods, especially at night, lying in bed in the dark, wide awake and unable to let go of the careening thoughts in my head. Eventually, worn down by endless musing, sleep won out. Learning to stop ruminating was an early first step in preventing a slide into self-doubt.

Two more techniques I learned early were very important. One was to notice my breathing, and to pay attention to drawing breath in and letting it out. The instruction was to "bring awareness to the breath." The point was to become aware of the breath carrying oxygen to all the parts of my body. It sounds overly simplistic. However, over time, taking a few moments to focus on breathing, even in the midst of a busy day, when negative thoughts were starting to happen, became an important way to interrupt the downward spiral of negative thinking.

My third resource was the discovery that thoughts are not things. They are products of my mind. I can prevent them from taking over simply by deciding not to follow them. When a negative thought about myself or an experience occurs, I can choose to let it go, rather than letting it occupy my attention. It is important not to judge or criticize myself because a negative thought comes to mind. In fact, it is essential that I treat myself with non-judgmental kindness by doing no more than noticing that a negative thought has occurred, and then letting it go. The kindness to self lies in the act of letting negative thoughts go just as quickly as they enter.

Clearly, the benefits of mindfulness are gained only by spending time with specific practices of self-awareness. I learned them not only through reading, but also by attending a class taught by Dr. A. It involved eight two-hour sessions spread over the same number of weeks. The group was small, and the participants were committed to attending all of the sessions.

Dr. A. is trained in the mindfulness-based approach to the treatment of depression. There was great benefit in being able to experience the practices of mindfulness with a group of individuals who also were dealing with depression and anxiety. Sharing with others and hearing the feelings they experienced in doing these practices also are important elements in the process of recovery. It was helpful to know I was not alone in learning to be mindfully aware and thus able to counter the habits of mind which contribute to depression.

ANATOMY OF A MOOD SWING

From time to time in the journey of confronting depression, I could feel what I called a "down time," or a mood swing, coming on. After one such experience, I wrote a narrative about its beginning stages and the action which caused it to begin to lift.

> *Yesterday, Tuesday, March 11, 2014 brought a beautiful sunshine day, and I worked in the shop for a couple of hours. After I closed the shop, I took a long walk, about thirty minutes. I felt good when I got home. We had dinner, and Ginny went to her meeting. Later, we watched TV until 11:00 p.m. About an hour before bed, I took three mini aspirins, hoping this would help me sleep and reduce the effects of my cold.*

> *The next morning, I finally woke up at 7:30 a.m. after a fitful night in which I was awake several times. I went to my meeting at church at 10:00 a.m. The drive home was gray. The sky was threatening the promised rainstorm. When I got home, Ginny had baked the cookies she promised for a friend's party. She needed to deliver them, and I rode along. We arrived at the friend's house, a fascinating, very distinctive place. We ended up with a cook's tour that lasted an hour. Tired, we left at 1:45 p.m. and decided to get lunch. We were back home about 3:15 p.m. I planned to call the doctor's office for an*

appointment for my pre-op physical check-up, which
I needed prior to my shoulder surgery. I made the call
and set the date.

Now fatigue set in, and I sat down to watch TV.
After less than an hour, I gave up. The darkening
skies made the day grayer, and I really was in a
'down' mood. I knew that going to the woodshop
wasn't an option until the warm weather returned
later in the week. Remembering I needed to look at
materials for my mindfulness class, I went upstairs
and read the week's assignment, then tried a three-
minute breathing exercise. It was half-hearted. I read
the lines about not being able to think my way out of
depression, but having to act my way out. I decided
to write about the last 36 hours and the swing from
the high after the woodshop fun yesterday to the low
at the end of today. I heard Ginny start to prepare
supper, and I went to join her. Now that supper and
doing dishes are over, I'm finishing this little writing
project before I watch any more TV. The 'down'
mood seems to have lifted.

I share this story because it illustrates the truth that I cannot think my way out of depression. My "down" mood did not really begin to change and lift until I made the conscious decision to do an active thing. The practices outlined above also were helpful, but activity did the real work. In the months and years since that experience, there have been periodic occasions when I have been able to interrupt the negative mood more quickly than was the case earlier.

Being aware of and using the various practices of mindfulness have been essential elements in the process of overcoming my depression and caring for the little boy who is my inner child. He no longer feels lost. Even though much of the pain of my childhood trauma had been confronted and healed with the help of Dr. A. and mindful awareness, several stressful elements of my childhood experience were still in need of healing.

Dealing with Post-Traumatic Stress (PTS)

Nearing the end of my long-term work in therapy, the focus turned to specific unresolved issues. I continued to feel regret, and wished that this painful childhood experience had not happened. In addition, I still was struggling with the question of how to forgive myself, an issue which also is connected with shame. Dr. A. reminded me again that I had experienced childhood trauma. She saw my lingering pain and grief as aspects of Post-Traumatic Stress. She suggested I see a clinician whose practice included a specific focus on treating Post-Traumatic Stress using EMDR therapy. The acronym stands for Eye Movement Desensitization and Reprocessing. This is a technique developed fairly recently in the practice of psychotherapy. It is intended to relieve the distress connected with traumatic memories. I made an appointment in the spring of 2017.

Before describing the next part of the story, it is important to recall the incident described in the previous chapter when Dad took my brother Frank and me to the hospital to see Mom. In that session, I recalled entering the hospital and going to Mom's room. At the end of that retelling of the trip, Dr. A. asked me why I thought Dad had taken us to see Mom. My reply was that I thought he feared she might die. As soon as I acknowledged this, the intensity of the pain of that moment overwhelmed me, and the words burst out as if I was there again. *No! No! I don't want Mommy to die. Mommy, you can't die!"* I don't recall that I said them out loud at the time, but they had erupted out loud in my answer to the question.

In the following session, Dr. A. again asked me to recall the visit with Mom, but this time to focus on recalling as best I could our leaving the hospital. Following her questions, I related again the events of the experience. They were unchanged, but my sense of color in the hospital corridors was somewhat different until I reached Mom's room. The sense of the room being white was the same as in the earlier recollection. This time I did not sense emotion, but I had little interest in being in the room. It seemed we left the hospital by the same route as in the previous experience. I sensed wanting to leave quickly. At first, after this guided revisit, it seemed there was nothing significantly different from the first experience.

However, in this session with Dr. A. my mind flipped to an image of Dad and me in the car. Suddenly, I was the child on the way home from the hospital. I was gripped with a sudden yearning. I was powerless to quell the eruption of emotion and tears as they welled up. Without any thought, the words blurted out: "*I want my Mommy back. I just want my Mommy I used to have back.*"

After several moments of stress, the tears and grief again eased. I was awed by the intensity of the childhood feelings that had surfaced from the ride in the car after the visit to Mom. After so many years had passed, the deep recesses of my brain still could relive the power of those feelings.

These two incidents about the visit to my Mom were part of the background I provided in my first two sessions with the PTS specialist. I also had described for her the experience of standing by myself in the large social hall of our church and feeling alone, and not wanting to sit with the couple I sat with in church when Mom was not there.

In the third session with the therapist dealing with PTS, she asked if I would be open to taking part in a session of EMDR therapy. I agreed. Without describing it in detail, it involved a period of focusing on and following a series of lights. She asked if I was willing to revisit an event I mentioned in the two introductory sessions. I agreed.

The therapist asked me to close my eyes if I wished, and imagine myself in a very comfortable, safe and serene place, any place I wished to choose. She suggested I select a person or animal or object that I would see as my defender. She also asked me to visualize a person or animal or object that would be my absolute source of nurture and care. I thought about a woman who felt like a second mother to me, especially in my early teen years.

From my earlier summary of events around my mother's illness, the therapist asked me to try to go back to my experience on a Sunday I previously described. Normally, I sat with my mother during church, unless she was playing the piano for the young children. But during her illness and beyond, after I attended my Sunday School class, I usually sat during church service with Mr. and Mrs. Bailey, in the pew they frequently occupied near the back of the church. I've never forgotten their names.

The event I was asked to revisit occurred in the basement of the church in a large open area called the undercroft. It was a space for large gatherings. It featured four slender, fluted white columns arranged well apart from each other, forming a large rectangle. Each was the same distance from the corners of the room. I don't remember the color of the walls, although I associate white with the ceiling. I remembered specifically standing alone in the middle of that big open space after Sunday School class. Now, in this session, the therapist asked me to follow the lights. After stopping them, she asked,

"What comes up for you."

Sunday school was over. Daddy was somewhere else in church. I was supposed to go up to the sanctuary to sit with the Baileys.

Again, I followed the lights and then: "What comes up for you?"

They're okay. I just have to sit with them. They let me draw doodles on the worship bulletin.

"What comes up for you?"

I really didn't want to sit with them. They're okay, but I miss my Mom. I want to be with my Mom! I really don't want to go upstairs.

There were several more sets of lights followed by my expressions of thoughts, emotions and feelings. In the process, the intensity of my pain began to diminish.

"What is coming up?"

I really just want to go home.

"Who do you want to take you home?"

My caring person.

"OK. Your caring person has taken you home. And you walk in the front door.

What comes up?"

I don't really know. I don't remember anything in particular. My grandmother (Mommy's Mom) or my great aunt was there because my

175

younger brothers were home. I guess I just kind of went off to play on my own.

After allowing a few moments for some of the intensity of this experience to pass, the therapist guided me back to the present. She commented about the recollection that my imagined arrival home was followed by my simply going off to play. She felt that it was an indication that in the real situation, the adult at home would have been occupied with the care of my younger siblings. This wasn't an intentional desire to isolate me.

In the follow-up review of this episode, the therapist asked me who my safe person was I wanted to take me home. It was the wife of the director of youth programming for our denomination's churches in Ohio. I knew her from attending many youth conferences and having visited her home. I also had helped her as she cared for her baby one weekend. In choosing her, I was recalling a person who I knew loved me without reservation. She seemed to know I wanted to be close.

Although the therapist asked me to imagine the outcome of going home, the reality was that I remained at church and must have gone up to the sanctuary on my own to find the Baileys. However, the recollected pain of standing in the undercroft, the large social hall in the church's lower level, and wanting my absent mother was intensely real.

We talked about my feelings in response to the guided visit back to that lonely, big empty space of the social hall. It felt to me, in the present with the therapist, as if my six-year-old self finally had been able to tell someone of my loneliness and yearning for my Mom. The intensity of the anguished feelings of aloneness startled me. Again, I had not known there was so much buried pain. I suspect that the episode of being alone in that big space of the undercroft actually took place on a Sunday after my father took me and my brother to see Mom in the hospital. That visit, and the feelings and fears associated with them, only intensified my anguish over my absent mother. Over all the years between that Sunday morning in 1944 and a therapy session in 2017, my mind held onto the picture of me standing alone in that big room.

I've only recently learned about the capacity of the brain to retain permanently the emotional pain involved in traumatic experiences, even though such pain may be repressed from immediate memory. It took hard work to realize and accept the meaning of my mental image of standing alone in that place, unable to be near my Mom.

The therapist explained to me that one of the realities of my experience is that my parents, and most of those who knew me, were unable to recognize and validate my feelings and emotions in reaction to my mother's illness. **Such a lack of recognition of a child's emotions, can be as detrimental as physical or verbal abuse. This is one of the reasons separating children from their parents as an element of immigration policy is such a tragic and inhumane policy, inflicting long-term psychological damage.** One person in my life who I believe sensed my emotions was Keever, the woman from the church office who took me to the circus one day and bought me a red balloon.

Ultimately, the referral for special treatment of my Post-Traumatic Stress has enabled me to overcome the deep grieving which was attached to the traumatic separation from my Mom. That work, together with the long therapeutic journey with Dr. A., has given me profound insights into the psychology of my life and the family which nurtured me. The childhood experiences of "Little Rob," once locked away as terribly painful events, no longer have the power to manifest the grief and pain they once did. The events of long ago have become accepted elements of my life story and part of who I am today.

Occasionally, I wish some aspects of my life had been different, but I choose to live in the present. As I write this, I know there is still some work to do to address the difficulty of overcoming these moments of regret. Occasionally, the sense of shame I tried to bury, for years, rears up. The process for healing it, is the subject of the next chapter.

The past is over and gone. My desire is to live today for today. Yes,

I make plans for doing those things which interest me. I try to keep them realistic. The whole story of my life is not yet written, and I now can accept and honor my life, with more to come.

NOTES

1. Bradshaw, Joh Eliot, *Homecoming: Reclaiming and Championing Your Inner Child,* (New York, Bantam Books, 1990).

2. Williams, Teasdale, Segal and Kabat-Zinn, Op. Cit., p.19.

Chapter 12

Overcoming Shame:
The Challenge of Self-Acceptance

PERHAPS THE MOST DIFFICULT CHALLENGE HAS BEEN TRYING TO COPE WITH THE DEEP REGRET I HAVE FELT ABOUT THE DARKEST ASPECTS OF THIS EXPERIENCE. These are the moments of wishing I did not become addicted to alcohol and that it was not true that I was unfaithful in my first marriage. Perhaps the deepest regret of all has been that I was not emotionally equipped to deal effectively with the responsibilities I had trained for and been ordained to live out. The nagging question has been: "How can I heal the shame I feel for falling short of the high calling I had accepted for my life?" Yes, I achieved the external educational requirements and developed many of the skills required of a pastor. It was the emotional intelligence that was impaired, the ability to understand what was influencing my deep feelings of being disconnected from those I love and driving my misguided need to be in control. This was a fact I did not understand until the years of my formal career had passed and my psyche let go of the buried grief and pain during that fateful first session with Dr. A.

I've learned there are two kinds of shame. One is the shame and embarrassment which come from committing a significant error in judgment, or being caught in breaking a norm of behavior. A person is usually able to readily atone for such infractions. Often an apology is required as well as asking to be forgiven, or an individual causes an accident which harms another and, feeling shame, seeks a means for making the injured party whole. Obviously, this is the kind of shame which results from many of the behaviors which occur when one's inhibitions are lowered under the influence of alcohol. In my experience, perfunctory apologies for my behavior when intoxicated were insufficient either to right the wrong that may have occurred, or to heal the shame. It was only after accepting the fact of my addiction, my powerlessness over alcohol, that I was able to accept the help of others and begin the road to recovery.

The second form of shame is deeper, and threatens one's well-being and sense of worth as a person. This is the shame that says "my life is not worthy," or "I am not worthy as a person." This is the shame that causes a person to doubt he or she merits love, and to doubt that there is meaning or purpose for that person's being. This is the kind of shame that leads individuals to feel unacceptable to themselves, to others or even to God.

In the course of my work with Dr. A., I sorted through the feelings of self-criticism about actions which caused my feelings of shame. In the early years of being sober, I made amends to many people as I lived through the steps toward living into sobriety. Even so, it was the self-criticism, what Dr. A. called my "inner critic," which continued to view me as an unworthy person. She felt that this "inner critic" was not the making of some recent event or experience, but rather came from some deeply-held, long-ago experience.

As I've thought about this and tried to uncover its source within my deepest feelings, I sense that it came from multiple sources. One obviously is the deeply-imbedded, but erroneous, childhood belief that my mother, in some unfathomable and unexplainable way, had rejected me. That was a perception I had to ignore and press on, coping as best I could. A second source of the inner critic seems to me to have been the childhood expectation that one day I would achieve a highly successful career, one which would measure up to that of grandfather Caris' achievement as a college president and grandfather Peters' success as a college pastor and denominational leader. My father's career and achievements clearly were part of this dynamic. As I have mentioned, I grew up with the expectation that we boys would pursue professions which contribute to the common good.

My self-criticism and shame were also influenced by other expectations expressed from our earliest days. This is different from the question of whether I am able to accept the events in my personal story. It involves recognizing ways in which my parents, especially my father, wanted his family to be an upstanding model of success and deportment, to use an old-fashioned term I often heard from my grade-school principal. There were many ways in which Dad tried to protect us from the consequences of making mistakes and assure that we did not do things which might reflect negatively on, or tarnish, the image of a successful family. In some instances, we needed to be allowed to discover consequences for ourselves. We were especially aware of his concern for proper behavior when we were attending events at church.

We also learned fairly early that expressions of emotion or feelings were to be controlled. Expressions of anger among us boys were not allowed. I do not recall our parents ever raising their voices. The fact that we were not a family which outwardly exhibited affection contributed to my feelings of isolation and a sense that something was missing from our home.

The concern to put forward a positive image was expressed to me directly at the time Dad decided to accept a call to a new pastorate in 1958. The person he followed in that pulpit apparently left amid questions of inappropriate conduct. I was in college at the time, and distinctly recall Dad telling me that he had accepted the call, in part, because he felt our family could provide a model of a stable family for the congregation. Similarly, many times when Dad introduced the family to someone, he would make a particular point of noting that he and Mom had grown up in Defiance and attended college there, noting that "Mary's father was president of the college in the 1920s and 1930s." This clearly was a marker from the family heritage which helped him have a sense of identity. It was a source of family pride conveyed to us boys as well. When we were in college, Mom and Dad were proud to mention, and rightfully so, the colleges we were attending.

As we grew older, both in college and beyond, each of us encountered our own difficulties and demons. These became serious challenges to our ability to live well and to be successful in our chosen careers and professions. Increasingly, when asked about how each of us was getting along, our parents had to gloss over the real struggles each of was having. Similarly, as each of us faced these challenges, we found it necessary to share less of our real situations.

A remembrance of each of my brothers appears in the last chapter. The reflections are my way of acknowledging and affirming them in the midst of the emotional challenges we all faced. As the only survivor of my own generation and heir to my parents' generation, I want Frank and Alan and Gregory to have their rightful places in the story. I want to acknowledge the ways in which the family crisis was a major influence in the crises each of them experienced. At the same time, each of them was a unique and loved person. Writing these remembrances helps me see and cherish the reality of my family apart from the idealized perceptions of my youth.

"FROM THE GUT" SHAME

Whatever the source of my inner critic, I continued to struggle with the questions: "How could I dare let anyone know the reality of my past?" "How could I openly accept and acknowledge the whole of my experience?" It seemed that if the truth of my life were known, no one would see me as a worthy person, even though I was able to overcome the darkness in my life, emerge into a long and committed marriage and be accepted among clergy friends.

The experience of shame has a corrosive effect on self-esteem. More than that, it creates deep-seated grief and an inability to forgive one's self for that which is deemed to be the "bad" aspects of one's life. This, in the end, was the hardest challenge of all. How could it be possible to arrive at the place where I could forgive myself for what I deemed the "bad," even unforgiveable, elements of my life? The issue was made more difficult by the fact that my religious background taught me there are certain immutable rules, yes "commandments," which are not to be broken. My mind and understanding said they had been broken, so that self-forgiveness and healing became a seemingly impossible challenge, even if much of my behavior had stemmed from a childhood trauma which disrupted healthy emotional growth and development.

This was the ultimate challenge in the therapeutic process which began in the summer of 2009 with such profound pain and sadness. If I was ever to be an emotionally secure and truly happy person, then I would have to heal this deep-seated sense of unworthiness, what my PTS specialist calls a "from-the-gut" feeling. Somehow, the "inner critic" had to be disarmed so that it no longer would have the power to control my self-perception and my ability to accept the reality of my life.

Both my PTS therapist and Dr. A. provided tools which helped me find the sources of my grief and loss and understand the emotional absence of my Mom. They helped me see the broken places in my life in the context of a struggle to survive emotionally. They helped me befriend the little boy who thought his Mom didn't want him anymore. And now they were giving me the resources to disempower this life-destroying shame and find reconciliation and forgiveness for myself.

FINDING RADICAL SELF-ACCEPTANCE

One of the resources given to me was a recorded presentation by Dr. Tara Brach, a noted clinical psychologist and teacher of mindfulness. Her approach included ideas drawn from Buddhist perspectives on meditation. The audio disc is titled *Radical Self-Acceptance: A Buddhist Guide to Freeing Yourself from Shame (1)*. Dr. Brach helped me see that my own effort to wish away the "bad" experiences is exactly the way to reinforce the feelings of shame. My negative inner critic was only making the feeling of self-reproach worse. Contrary to what one might think, the key to dis-empowering shame is being able to acknowledge the presence of what I want to reject, and seeing it with what mindfulness practice calls "kind awareness."

Brach points out that many people, just as I was prone to do, want to avoid any sense of deficiency in their lives. We seek many different ways to run from our shame, or to try to conform with expectations in order to please others, and thus feel better. Addiction is one means of fleeing from shame, as is denial of our negative experiences. The effort to cover up, or to overcome, what we perceive as deficiency only increases the shame. Conversely, welcoming with kindness what is in our lives becomes the avenue for beginning to heal.

Brach goes on to describe the importance of our connectedness to one another. She highlights what it means to live in harmony with one another, and to learn to be without anxiety about our imperfections. In the course of the recorded sessions, she provides guided mediations. These enable the listener to experience being with what is painful and difficult in new ways, and thus develop the sense that we belong to the whole of creation.

The meditations helped me begin to see how my sense of who I am is very much dependent on my connections with other people and the larger world. One of Dr. Brach's comments which touched me most deeply was the idea that healing can result from being part of loving relationships because they offer the space to be open to myself. In the final session of her presentation, Dr. Brach addresses spiritual practices as an element of being connected to the entire web of life. The focus is on our inter-connectedness with the earth and creation. Being sensitive to the needs and concerns of others becomes a part of our healing and restoration to fulness of living. To me, these are essential elements of spiritual practice, regardless of the religious tradition within which one lives. Dr. Brach and my therapists opened the way to dis-empowering the shame I harbored for so long.

The Value of Two Careers

Not long after Dad was diagnosed with the cancer which would end his life, we had a conversation in which he wondered out loud what his career had been worth. In effect, his question was "Has my career been of any real value?" He began to list his pastorates and what had happened to those congregations in the years following his time with each one. The congregation he served immediately after seminary did not become part of the United Church of Christ when it was established in 1957. Park Street Congregational Church in Bridgeport, Connecticut, a large congregation he left in 1947 when he was called to Sandusky, shrank until it could not survive and merged with another congregation. By 1990, First Congregational Church in Sandusky declined from more than five hundred members during his tenure to roughly two hundred twenty-five.

"Sometimes," he said, "I wonder if my career accomplished anything."

I pointed out to him that his career and ministry were worth a great deal to the people he served in each of his positions. "Your ministry," I said, "has been about the pastoral care of all those babies you blessed in baptism, all those couples whose weddings you rehearsed and conducted, the families you comforted as they mourned and all the folks who came to worship Sunday after Sunday. Your years of ministry were not about buildings and organizations. They were about the people whose lives were enriched because you were there and responded when they needed you."

In the present moment as I write these words, I suddenly hear them as the summation of the worth of my own ministry as well as my Dad's. In the end, by the grace of God and the help of both therapists and friends, I have come through the challenges and developed a new perspective which allows me to see the value of the whole of my experience and my family's story. My work with philanthropic agencies and consulting with churches has been a worthy ministry in its own right. The word philanthropy comes from two Greek words: *philein*, to love, and *anthropos*, meaning man or humanity. To engage in philanthropy is to be involved with love for humanity. The concepts of ministry and philanthropy are closely linked. I have been privileged to serve both.

Today I am able to see my career not only in terms of emotional recovery, but also in terms of spiritual rebirth, the subject of the next chapter.

NOTES

1. Brach, Tara: *Radical Self-Acceptance: A Buddhist Guide to Freeing Yourself from Shame,"* on compact disk, (Boulder, Co, Sounds True, 2000).

Chapter 13

Spiritual Rebirth

M Y SPIRITUAL REBIRTH COULD NOT HAVE HAPPENED WITHOUT FIRST ACKNOWLEDGING THAT I WAS ADDICTED TO ALCOHOL. That was the beginning, the first stage of reviving my spirituality. To my mind, it is significant that more than twenty years of growing into sobriety went by before my deeply-buried emotions and the broken childhood connection with my Mom could surface and trigger the effort to seek help in psychotherapy.

Today, I choose to say I am powerless over alcohol. I cannot predict how much alcohol I might consume after the first drink. I might have enough control to say "one is enough," but I could just as easily feel like another wouldn't hurt me and then quickly be into the urge for more. Using alcohol for more than twenty years produced a variety of effects. One is that it quickly became a way to make painful and uncomfortable experiences feel less so. In my late twenties and thirties, it limited the development of emotional awareness and sensitivity. It also impaired my ability to anticipate the consequences of decisions and my ability to manage the stresses of life. A fourth effect was the well-known capacity of alcohol to cloud one's judgment and remove inhibitions which would, for a sober person, serve to prevent making decisions likely to result in negative, if not harmful, consequences. Impacted by these realities, I now also believe that what spirituality I could muster was severely limited by an inability to be fully attentive to spiritual practice. My involvement with alcohol impaired my ability to engage in an active spirituality.

The second stage of my spiritual rebirth has been the process of discovering, through sustained work with a skilled therapist sensitive to the spiritual dimensions of life, a whole new way of understanding and experiencing spirituality. In one of our early sessions, Dr. A. wondered if I had experienced meditation. I had not, other than to be reflective in relation to some of the spoken and printed prayers during the course of Sunday worship. I also recalled my earliest experience with the practice of morning watch at summer church youth camp. Dr. A. is a person of faith, and has a profound understanding of the place of meditation in the spiritual life.

From our work, she knew that my spiritual life through most of my adult years after parish ministry had been nurtured by being a member of a local congregation and participating in the ordinary forms and words of weekly Sunday worship. She understood the spiritual dryness I was experiencing. She also understood the likelihood that I would continue to experience times of stress and depression in coming weeks.

Over the course of our work, she shared with me two resources which would prove invaluable for helping me cope not only with my spiritual life, but also with the "down" times and the requirements of ongoing daily life as I began a time away from therapy. The first resource completely changed my understanding of spiritual growth. Amazingly, it is an approach to prayer I did not know, in spite of my professional training and initial career. Dr. A. suggested I get a copy of a book by Cynthia Bourgeault, an Episcopal priest, and a writer about developing the spiritual life. She has long experience as a student and teacher in Benedictine monasteries and spiritual retreats. Her book, Centering Prayer and Inner Awakening (1), provided an in-depth introduction to the ancient practices and methodologies of Christian contemplative prayer. I was astonished by what I found.

TOWARD DIVINE AWARENESS

Bourgeault uses a model, attributed to Father Thomas Keating, which illustrates the ways in which we experience awareness (2). It consists of three concentric rings. Each one represents a level of a person's awareness.

The first level, the outer-most ring, represents "ordinary awareness," our usual way of thinking about and describing the everyday world. Bourgeault provides a wonderful description of the ways in which ordinary awareness intrudes on our minds, thus preventing us from

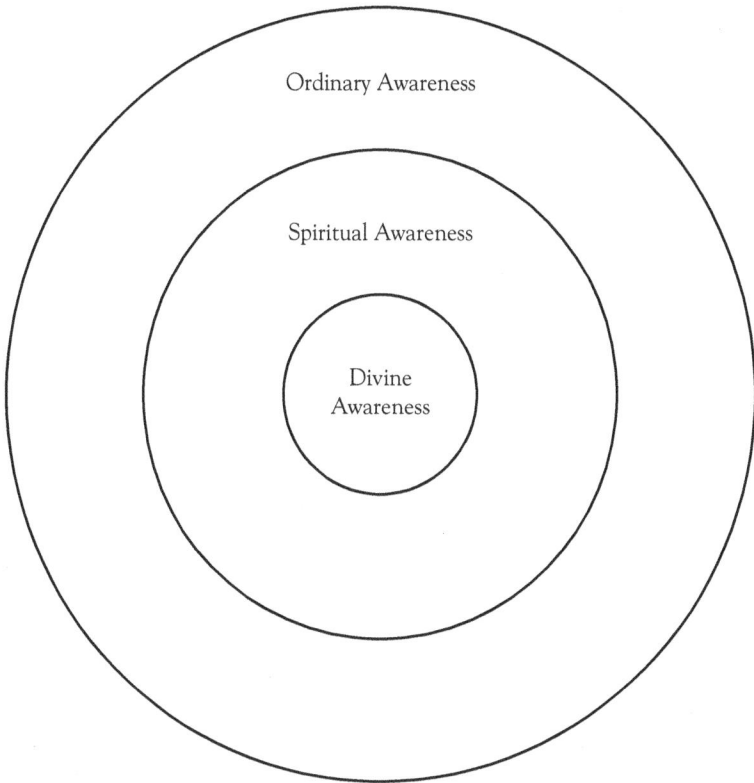

Ordinary Awareness

Spiritual Awareness

Divine
Awareness

concentrating on one idea for any length of time. A thought is easily
distracted by another. Teachers of spirituality like to refer this phenomenon
as "monkey mind," because our minds jump from thought to thought, not
lingering long on any one.

The second ring, located inside the first, is called "spiritual awareness."
It also is a way of perceiving, but it is more like having the sense of
something greater than ourselves. It comes to us in such moments as seeing
an amazing landscape or hearing great music which fills us with awe.

The third ring is inside the second and represents "divine awareness."
It is a place deep within us, wherein we meet what may be called the "divine
indwelling." The following brief passage captures the essence of this idea.

> As we move toward center, our own being
> and the divine being become more and more
> mysteriously interwoven. 'There is in the soul a
> something in which God dwells, and there is in
> the soul a something in which the soul dwells in

189

God,' writes the medieval mystic Meister Eckert,
the subtlety of his words reflecting the delicacy of
the motion (3).

Bourgeault explores this theological and spiritual truth in greater depth and includes insights from the modern mystic Thomas Merton. She shares her own affirmation: "The divine indwelling is the cornerstone of contemplative prayer." The Apostle Paul offers a glimpse of this insight in the third chapter, verses 18 and 19 of his letter to the church at Ephesus:

> 18 I pray that you may have the power to
> comprehend, with all the saints, what is the
> length and breadth and height and depth, 19
> and to know the love of Christ that surpasses
> knowledge, *so that you may be filled with all the
> fulness of* God (4). *(italics added)*

This notion, that the intention of contemplative prayer is to be in the presence of the Divine, not as a being far off, but as a presence within one's own being, completely altered my sense of what spirituality can be about. The realization has revived and reshaped my spiritual life.

Bourgeault focuses on two ancient approaches to the practice of Christian meditation and the contemplative life. The first is a way of reading and praying about passages of scripture. It is known by its Latin term: *lectio divina*. These two words literally mean "reading the sacred." This is an approach long known to monks and contemplatives as an intentional way to engage in study and prayer about the scriptures.

The second approach to prayer, known as "centering prayer," is an approach to contemplation without using words, or the ordinary faculties of thought, memory, or imagination. First, it is important to address the practice of reading the scriptures.

Lectio Divina

This is a method of reading and entering into meditation about a relatively brief passage of scripture, perhaps six to twelve lines, although a reader may focus on a longer passage. *Lectio divina* consists of four stations.

Bourgeault suggests the term "stations" rather than "stages," to refer to the four parts of this approach to experiencing the scriptures. The word "stages" conveys the idea that each part is distinct from the others. The difficulty with the word "stages" is that it suggests a ladder-like, ascending progression, instead of a circular sequence of stations, where each is its own aspect of the total contemplative experience. No station is seen as being higher or lower in importance than another, as is the case in a hierarchy. This idea also avoids the suggestion that only a limited few contemplatives are ever able to reach the "highest" level of contemplative experience. Overall, the practice of *lectio divina* leads one to each of these stations in an ever-deepening experience with the chosen text.

The Latin words for each of the stations are the root words for their counterparts in English. The stations are *lectio* (to read, lection), *meditatio* (to meditate), *oratio* (to speak, as in prayer), and *contemplatio* (to contemplate, as in a deep awareness of the divine). The following paragraphs provide a brief description of each station of this approach to reading and being with a passage of scripture.

Lectio (lection) is the root word of lectionary, the term used to describe the listings of scripture readings for each Sunday of the church year. The first station of *lectio divina* is to read the chosen passage of scripture. It is read slowly three times, preferably out loud, so that one can hear the variations in meanings that occur when hearing the text. With each reading, the suggestion is to change the pace and emphasis, noticing the variations of meaning which may occur. One listens for the word or simple phrase which calls for extra attention. The reader is invited to consider the ways in which changing the emphasis on this word affects the meaning of the passage.

Meditatio (meditation) After hearing the words, begin to ask questions of the passage. What did the writer mean to convey? Could there be more than one way to understand the text? What unwritten assumptions are behind the passage? How does it speak to you? What feelings does the passage bring up? Does this passage say anything about the love of God for you or for the wider world? You may form your own questions as you consider and meditate about the chosen passage.

Oratio (oration, speaking) This is a station in which one offers to God prayers expressed in words. Here a person begins to experience whatever feelings the text may bring up, acknowledging them in the presence of God. In this portion of the prayer, the process moves from the head and thinking into the heart and the feelings which the text may generate. For many who are accustomed more to thinking about faith, paying attention to feelings evoked by a passage may be a more difficult aspect of this approach to prayer. Most of us tend to be more interested in the thinking aspect of faith than in the feeling dimensions. The text may lead us to a feeling experienced by a person in the text, or it may trigger a feeling in ourselves. Whatever feeling comes up, simply notice it. It may be happiness or joy, love or doubt, whatever it may be, simply notice it. Gradually, the third station moves us into the realm of feelings and the realm of the heart.

Prayer from the heart, not the head, is challenging for most Western Christians. An ancient collection of spiritual writings from Eastern Christianity, contrasted with Western, or Roman Christianity, is called the Philokalalia. It calls the reader to "Put the mind in the heart…put the mind in the heart… stand before the Lord with the mind in the heart." The movement in this direction draws one toward the fourth station, *contemplatio.*

Contemplatio (contemplation) This is prayer without words. The fourth station gives us entry to the method of prayer which will enable us to learn to "stand before the Lord with the mind in the heart." We simply wait on the presence of God. This is the part of *lectio divina* which is the most challenging for many. As humans, we are used to doing the work of our egos – running things, doings things, trying to improve the condition of our lives. In short, we are trying to satisfy the demands of what psychologists call our egoic selves. However, contemplation calls us to let all of that go, and simply to be in the moment.

It's not easy to enter silence. The purpose is not to try to empty our minds. This is not possible. Minds think, all the time. The challenge in contemplation is to let thoughts go by, only noticing that a thought has come to us, and then immediately let it float away, like a boat going down a river, or like a cloud drifting away. Instead of dwelling on it when a thought occurs, one uses a sacred word to return to silence and contemplation. The concern is that one not worry that thoughts happen, but to see them only as opportunities to leave them behind and return to the presence of God.

This fourth station of *lectio divina* is an opportunity to be in silence, to be open to the presence of the divine within us. Contemplation is an experience of waiting for God to come to us in whatever way God may choose to be present. In the context of *lectio divina*, contemplation takes place after focusing the attention on a particular passage of scripture. By engaging the scriptures through regular practice of *lectio divina*, one will begin to know the scriptures with greater depth and vibrancy.

SILENCE AND CENTERING PRAYER

Bourgeault provides a model for understanding the place of Centering Prayer in an individual's spiritual development. She quotes the mystic John of the Cross who wrote that "Silence is God's first language" (5). She speaks of "different kinds of silence," an outer silence, "an outer stopping of words and busy-ness" and "a much more challenging inner silence where the inner talking stops as well" (6). This intentional silence, or meditation, is directed toward freeing our minds from words and thoughts. Centering Prayer is a way of entering into contemplation without using words or the ordinary faculties of thought, memory, imagination, written or spoken words. The term for this type of prayer is "apophatic." It is prayer that simply waits in silence for the presence of God. Our human tendency is to resist such a practice.

Achieving greater spiritual growth requires developing a regular practice of meditation to achieve greater spiritual awareness. Bourgeault suggests "ninety percent of the trick in establishing a successful practice lies in wanting to do it in the first place" (7). I have learned, over time, two primary aspects of the contemplative experience. The first is that when I maintain the daily discipline, I usually will spend, without a timer, a period of about twenty minutes engaged in silence, using the techniques for resisting the tendency to follow thoughts when they occur. The second, and frustrating reality, is that it is very easy to be distracted by the stresses of daily experience and thus fail to spend the time engaged in Centering Prayer. There isn't an easy motivator which prompts one to make the effort. The primary motivator is found in the progressive change in one's spiritual well-being and sense of nearness to the divine, which can only occur by observing the daily practice.

ENGAGING IN CENTERING PRAYER

Amazingly, the practice of centering prayer was forgotten in many Christian circles, with the exception of some monastic orders. It certainly remained unknown to lay people for centuries until the practice began to be revived in the 1970s. Although there has been a fairly widespread increase in interest about this method of prayer, I was completely unaware of it. Cynthia Bourgeault's work was like a deep breath of fresh air to a tired spirit whose practice had fallen into a rather lifeless go-through-the-motions observance.

Perhaps the easiest way to understand the impact of this way of prayer is to observe how it differs from the usual written and spoken prayers one encounters in Sunday worship. The contrast is especially sharp for me as a person who grew up in the Congregational branch of Protestantism. Most of the prayers in Sunday worship are printed in the Sunday bulletin or in the back pages of the hymnal. These prayers include, for example, prayers of invocation or prayers of confession, or of intercession on behalf of one's own needs or the needs of others. These are prayers which require us to use language, and the human faculties of imagination and memory to address our prayer to God. In virtually all cases, these are prayers in which the worshiper speaks to God, rather than listening for the presence of God. The prayers which use the human faculties of language and imagination and memory are called *cataphatic* prayers. Centering Prayer takes us away from the use of our human faculties and teaches us to let go of the thoughts which come to our minds. This is *apophatic* prayer, simply being in silence and letting the presence of God come into our hearts.

THE PRACTICE OF CENTERING PRAYER

For me, a time of centering prayer takes place in a quiet space where I am not likely to be interrupted. I like to sit in a comfortable straight back chair with my feet placed directly on the floor. My hands rest in my lap or on my thighs. I choose a word that is to be my sacred word. It can be any word which has a spiritual meaning for me. Some individuals prefer a brief phrase such as "hear my prayer," or "Lord, hear my prayer." The sacred word or phrase is used to return one's mind to the silence and refocus on being in the presence of the divine. When a thought crosses my mind, I only notice that it has happened and then let it drift away. I use the sacred word to return my attention to being in the presence of God. One should not criticize or judge one's self because the mind has followed a thought to somewhere far away. Simply use the sacred word to draw attention back to the silence.

As the number of times I engaged in centering prayer increased, the depth of the experience increased. A significant benefit of this contemplative experience is that it is available in the midst of whatever joy or difficulty is occurring in one's life. I also discovered that the more consistent I am in maintaining a daily time for meditation, the more it seems to fill a period of about twenty minutes. As one becomes more experienced, longer periods of silence become natural observances. There are simple timers which provide a soft bell or chime to signal the end of the desired length of time for meditation. Again, I do not let variations in the length of my meditation become occasions for judging whether I have engaged in it in a proper way. For me, part of the value of contemplative experience is that it is a way of being kind to myself.

One may legitimately ask the question: In what ways does *apophatic* (unspoken) *prayer* affect the contemplative person differently from the effect of more traditional *cataphatic* (spoken) prayer? The teachers of

Centering Prayer describe the ways in which this contemplative experience has positive psychological benefits in terms of contributing to inner healing. "Without a doubt, herein lies Thomas Keating's most profound contribution to contemporary spiritual psychology: in his recognition that Centering Prayer in some mysterious but undeniable way helps to initiate a process of psychological healing he calls the "Divine Therapy" (8). Bourgeault devotes two chapters to an extensive discussion of this phenomenon.

The Welcoming Prayer

An additional element of Centering Prayer is termed the Welcoming Prayer (9). This is prayer in which one simply welcomes the life situation which one is experiencing. The welcoming prayer is a way of acknowledging in the presence of God what currently is occurring in a person's life without expressing regret, anger or a wish that the situation was not present. This is not a prayer which absolves a person of responsibility to work to change the existing situation in one's life. Rather, it acknowledges to the divine what is real without engaging in pointless efforts to deny or rail against the reality in one's life.

Early in 2018, I was reminded of the power of this prayer in a personal situation. One evening, my wife and I returned from having dinner with friends. Through an unfortunate series of missteps, I fell to the concrete floor of the garage and broke my right femur below the hip joint. This resulted in a stay in the hospital for a surgical repair of the break. Three days later, I was transported to the healthcare facility in our retirement community for rehabilitation. For several days as an inpatient, I was deeply frustrated and resentful about having to endure this interruption of my daily routine and activities.

One, morning, during a time of reflection, I recalled the Welcoming Prayer as an element of contemplative prayer. In the quiet of my room, using my sacred word to interrupt thoughts and bring me back to the silence, I adopted an attitude of welcoming, rather than railing against, my situation. I let the reality of my injury and recovery process be the accepted truth of my situation, and did so in the mode of waiting upon the presence of God's love.

I was thankful that I was in a place where dedicated people were helping me recover. In the words of one of the wise adages in twelve-step programs, it was possible to "let go, and let God." For the most part, my controlling ego followed the words of the adage. The simple prayer was to ask God to continue to care for me, and that I continue to do the work of rehabilitation willingly and as well as I was able.

The Welcoming Prayer is more than a simple psychological acceptance of a real situation. It is a recognition that what is present in one's life can be experienced and accepted in the context of the unfailing love and presence of the Divine. The Welcoming Prayer removes resentment and complaint about one's life situation. It allows a spirit of cooperation and a willingness to pursue those actions which are available for doing what one can to live in the situation with grace.

Discovering Mysticism

The third step in my spiritual rebirth has been an unanticipated bonus from the discovery of Bourgealt's work on Centering Prayer. It has led me to the panoply of Christian mystics and the ancient treasure trove of knowledge and practice about the contemplative life. Bourgeault makes references to an unknown English monk in the late 14th century who wrote a treatise titled *The Cloud of Unknowing* (10). It is a primary source from which much of the technique for engaging in contemplative centering prayer was derived. The essence of its thesis is that God is hidden in a "cloud of unknowing." The contemplative person can only be in the presence of the divine by putting the normal process of thinking aside, and listening in silence for the presence of the Divine. Known by many as *The Cloud,* the treatise provides the rationale and the elements of apophatic, non- verbal, Centering Prayer. It is ironic that much of our electronic data now is stored in a "cloud" of a different sort, a "reality" the author of *The Cloud* could not have imagined.

Reading about *The Cloud* and its author started me on a quest to learn more about mysticism and the great mystics. An entire new world of spiritual experience and vision opened. This led to teaching a class in my congregation, focused on the lives of great Christian mystics. It began with the Desert Fathers and the Mothers of the second and third centuries, and continued with key figures of the medieval and contemporary eras. Not only were they profoundly spiritual leaders, but they also were deeply involved in the issues of the times. Modern examples include two Americans, Trappist monk Thomas Merton and Baptist minister Howard Thurman, and the Dutch priest Henri Nouwen, who wrote forty-one books on the nature and practice of spirituality.

One of Nouwen's themes is especially pertinent to my experience. It is a meditation based on Psalm 30, vss. 11 and 12. The psalmist rejoices for having had his health restored after facing death, and offers his praise to God and the promise of eternal gratitude. The *New Annotated Oxford Bible* translates these verses as follows:

11 You have turned my mourning into dancing;

> You have taken off my sackcloth
>
> And clothed me with joy,

12 So that my soul may praise you

> And not be silent,
>
> O Lord my God, I will give
>
> thanks to you forever.

The words "you have turned my mourning into dancing" powerfully express my own spiritual joy about the transformation in my life. In many ways, the long-buried sadness from misunderstanding what happened to me as the result of Mom's illness was a deep-seated mourning. Now that deep sadness has been changed into spiritual dancing, and a celebration of the unfailing presence of God's love.

Out of his darkest experiences and spiritual discipline, Nouwen became increasingly aware of the reality of God's compassion and love. He wrote about this love in his book, *Life of the Beloved* (11). The book is testimony to Nouwen's conviction that every person is beloved by God. This was a certainty for Nouwen, and it was central to his approach to understanding the spiritual life, and he wanted everyone with whom he came in contact to know this central fact of the whole of human experience as he understood it.

The spiritual awakening which came to Henri Nouwen in the words "You are the Beloved" is one with which I can identify in several ways. First, those words, as a reflection of divine love, provide reassurance that it is God's desire that broken relationships be restored. Second, these words remind me that the same unfailing love comes to me within my marriage. I live within a secure love, both in my spiritual relationship with God and in my most intimate personal relationship.

One of the dimensions of my spiritual rebirth is movingly portrayed in Nouwen's meditations on the parable of the Prodigal Son set forth in his book *The Return of the Prodigal Son: A Story of Homecoming* (12). This is a discussion of Nouwen's discovery of Rembrandt's painting *The Return of the Prodigal Son*. Having seen a copy of the painting on a poster during a trip to France, he resolved to go to Russia to the Hermitage to view the original painting. The chapters of the book focus on the meaning of the prodigal's return to each of the characters in the painting.

Rembrandt painted the event not as the original text describes it with the father rushing to meet the returning son. Rather the son, in tattered clothes, is kneeling before his father, in a scene painted with a dark background. The older son, partly in the shadows, looks on, and two lesser figures are barely visible deeper in the shadows. The bearded father is old and now nearly blind. The palms of his hands are on the upper back of the kneeling, penitent son. The scene conveys the emotions that come to me when I consider how my own journey has brought me back again to the source of my inspiration when I first recognized the call to ministry many decades ago. Nouwen wrote movingly about the father's compassion, and his willingness to let go of whatever anger or judgment he might have had toward his wayward son. Instead he is moved by joy and relief, indeed his unfailing love for his son and deep gratitude that his son has returned. The father is blessing his returned son.

Rediscovering a vital spirituality is, for me, similar to the prodigal's receiving anew God's unqualified blessing. It is the final step in the experience of overcoming shame and guilt. Nouwen understood God's love as a compassion which overcomes all human waywardness in the moment of the Prodigal's return. Reconciliation restores relationship with the Divine.

WOUNDED HEALER

Henri Nouwen also is the source of a notion about the meaning of ministry which resonates with me. His idea of the "wounded healer" connects with my own experience. His central idea is that ministers, as well as other practitioners who seek to help emotionally wounded people, must understand and work to heal their own wounds before they can be healers of those who come to them for help.

What does this mean? First, the minister needs to recognize that, for humans, loneliness is a painful condition which is a common experience. (13). Nouwen points out that each of us searches for unity and community and seeks various self-help strategies, therapies, and learning opportunities in an effort to overcome loneliness. In sum, Nouwen believes that within our deepest sense of ourselves we recognize that no human relationship has the capacity to overcome our feelings of being alone in the world. He says that for ministers, in particular, the loneliness is made greater by the relative low esteem in which members of the clergy are held by our society.

My own experience testifies to the truth of Nouwen's observations. Recall the distraught little boy in the midst of an empty large room, desperately wanting his missing mother. Go back to the loneliness of walking in the darkening, rain-soaked woods at Boy Scout Camp. Revisit my isolation when a romance failed; or the sense of unworthiness at the loss of a job, more than once. Recall the days of doubt in seminary, wondering if I should stay, or would be able to succeed in ministry. Remember with me the loneliness alcohol could not cure, and the isolating depression it helped to birth.

What steps can one take toward healing? As Nouwen sees it, one step is to view my loneliness as part of what all humans must experience. The task is not to complain about our situation to others. To do so is to engage in what Nouwen calls "spiritual exhibitionism." Instead, by understanding our inner pain, we recognize that we are connected to the same condition shared by every person. And the second step is to see that because we share this inner reality with all people, we are enabled to see and relate to others. Because we engage in this self-awareness, what Nouwen calls "introspection," we are able to offer hospitality to strangers. Thus, we are able to be open to the stranger who happens by. Nouwen points out that the Hebrew idea of hospitality allows us to hear and be open to the needs and concerns of others.

Nouwen reported an important observation by psychiatrist James Hillman of the C.G. Jung Institute in Zurich, Switzerland. Hillman observed that, to effectively approach the task of counseling an individual, the counselor must "withdraw" so as to "make room for the other." His insight is that this withdrawal, in the setting of counseling or therapy, allows the other person freedom to be open with the counselor.

This idea has profound meaning for me. I recognize in my therapist the depth of self-awareness which, in turn, allowed her to guide me to the depth of my own brokenness. To feel a renewed sense of ministry, as a "wounded healer," even though I am now in my eighties, is to have a larger capacity for being open to the needs and concerns of others, and a willingness to listen for their struggles at moments when they are open to sharing them. I am grateful for having discovered Nouwen's understanding of the "wounded healer." It reaffirms for me the reality that God restores and reconciles the prodigal to the Divine ever-present, healing love.

Outcomes

New understandings of prayer, the discovery of the great mystics, and lessons from such teachers as Cynthia Bourgeault and Henri Nouwen have carried me to a new level of spiritual awareness I did not know existed. The discovery of the mystics and their quest to be in the presence of the Divine and engaged with the world has brought new vitality to my life. I feel as if the mysterious, yet real presence of God I encountered during the candlelight meditation following the Service of Holy Communion at Camp Chafee so many years ago, is once again fully present to me. For me, the contemplative experience enriches participation in worship within the fellowship of a gathered community of the church. My spiritual journey has brought me back to the spiritual attachment with God I first sensed when I felt the call to ministry that summer evening, still vivid in my memory.

One morning, in the last stages of writing this memoir, an inspiration about the presence of God came to me. This poem was the result.

In the Warmth of God

Waking to the morning sun,
I'm wrapped in the warmth of God
knowing I am secure,
held in endless care
by an all-encompassing love.
It will not let me go,
though I may wander far from its
un-wavering compassion.
Broken by my egoic humanness,
and a child's mistaken belief
of mother's removed nurture,
I struggled back to find again
the dawning warmth of God.

The Return of the Prodigal Son painting by Rembrandt

NOTES

1. Bourgeault, Cynthia, Centering Prayer and Inner Awakening, (Lanham, Cowley Publications, 2004).

2. Ibid., p. 8.

3. Ibid., p. 13.

4. New Oxford Annotated Bible, (New York: Oxford University Press, 1991), p. 275 NT.

5. Bourgeault, op. cit. p.7.

6. Ibid., p. 7.

7. Ibid., p. 9.

8. Ibid., p. 39.

9. Ibid., p. 135.

10. Unknown Author, The Cloud of Unknowing, (Paulist Press, Mahwah, NJ, 1981).

11. Nouwen, Henri J.M., Life of the Beloved, (New York: Crossroad Publishing, 1992).

12. Nouwen, Henri J.M., The Return of the Prodigal Son: A Story of Homecoming, (New York: Image Books/Doubleday, 1994).

13. Nouwen, Henri, The Wounded Healer, (New York: Image/ Doubleday, 1979).

Chapter 14

Remembrances of My Brothers: The Rest of the Story

WRITING THIS MEMOIR HAS ENABLED ME TO SEE MORE CLEARLY THE POWERFUL DYNAMICS WHICH SHAPED MY FAMILY'S TRUE STORY AND TO ACCEPT BOTH ITS COMPLEXITY AND ITS REALITY. Clearly, my brothers were profoundly affected by our mother's illness. Because they were younger and did not have the same benefit of the more secure attachment I knew before she suffered her paralysis and long recovery, the after effects were substantially different for each of them. Gregory, having been born soon after her illness struck, suffered the greatest impact. My therapists have said that he had no opportunity to experience secure attachment in the immediate weeks after his birth. The result was a lifetime of difficult relationships and a struggle to discover a secure sense of himself. My brothers Alan and Frank faced challenges as well. The tributes in these pages are presented in the order in which my brothers died.

The remembrance of Gregory was written for this memoir. The other two were delivered during memorial services. There was no memorial service for Gregory. We three brothers and our wives were his only surviving family. Together with a cousin, we gathered at Byron Cemetery near Fairborn, Ohio in the spring of 2002 to inter his ashes in the plot shared by our parents. Portions of the Frank's and Alan's ashes are also interred there. These reflections acknowledge my brothers' struggles and achievements and honor their place in the generations and history of the family.

GREGORY PIERSON PETERS
FEBRUARY 2, 1944 – SEPTEMBER 20, 2001

Gregory was born at Bridgeport Hospital in Bridgeport, Connecticut. He faced challenges from the beginning due to our Mom's illness. During the early years of his life, I was not very aware of the nature of Greg's emotional relationship with Mom. To me, he was my little brother. When he was born, I was already in the first grade. His infancy and pre-school years were largely invisible to me because of the difference in our ages and daily routine. My clearest memories of him come from summer months around the time he was in the fourth to sixth grades. I seem to visualize him as a youngster who mostly played by himself, except for a best friend, a boy who lived across the street.

Then, in the summer of 1958, when Greg was fourteen and about to enter four-year high school in Sandusky, Dad became the minister at the Congregational Church in East Cleveland. We moved there, and in September Greg entered ninth grade at Kirk Junior High, a three-year middle school. A year later, he was uprooted again when he entered the three-year Shaw High School. A fourth disruption came a year and a half later when Dad accepted a position in New York. Mom stayed in East Cleveland, while Greg finished his junior year. Then in the October, when the East Cleveland church finally needed the parsonage, she and the household goods went to New York. Greg still had a year to finish at Shaw which he did by living with a next-door neighbor in East Cleveland. He graduated in June of 1962.

II

Following high school, he enrolled as a freshman at Yankton College, in South Dakota, a school which had a long-time connection with Congregational Churches. I think he was influenced in his choice by the woman who had been the Christian Education staff person at the church in East Cleveland. She was a graduate of Yankton. Unfortunately, at mid-year, Yankton College suddenly announced that it was closing its doors at the end of the school year. Uprooted again, Greg enrolled at Heidelberg College in Tiffin, Ohio in the Fall of 1963. He graduated there in June of 1966.

While writing this chronology, a startling realization has come to me. Gregory experienced a seemingly unending series of losses in the course of the first twenty-two years of his life. They began on the day of his birth, when he was whisked away from his mother to the hospital's nursery. Moreover, my brothers have told me that Greg said sometime during his youth that he believed he was the cause of Mom's illness when he was born. Though I have no way to prove it, my suspicion is that Greg developed this belief out of the magical thinking which psychologists tell us often occurs in young children near the age of six. When children experience or learn of bad things, they sometimes presume some action of theirs has caused the harmful event.

Beyond knowing of Mom's illness during his birth, Greg's experiences of being uprooted from the familiar in Sandusky, his school changes in East Cleveland, loss of family when Dad and Mom moved to New York while he stayed behind to finish his senior year in high school, and the disruption to his college education all were occasions for experiencing loss and forms of grief. The psychological impact surely was enormous.

He went on from Heidelberg College to complete a Master's Degree in Library Science at the University of Michigan. Then, over the next several years, until the mid-1980s, he was employed as a librarian in a variety of organizations. While still in college, his drinking began to be excessive. In the late 1980s, he lost the job he held with a publishing firm in Cincinnati. He never was employed again. For the balance of his life, he shared a house with a retired professor. He became totally dependent on his housemate and enabler for support.

III

In spite of many efforts to persuade Greg to enter addiction rehab, he would not consent. On September 16, 2001, a fall at home resulted in hospitalization. Tests revealed the dire condition of his health. With virtually no liver function and critical pulmonary disease, Greg was beyond recovery. Alan, Frank and I faced the logic of the situation two days earlier. We had agreed and advised the doctors that no heroic efforts should be made in a useless effort to prolong the inevitable. Greg could only be made comfortable for the brief span of life which remained. With all airplanes grounded after the terrorist attacks at the World Trade Center and the Pentagon, I drove to Cincinnati to meet Alan, who had come from Macon, Georgia. He and I saw Greg in the hospital.

Now, lying in a hospital bed, his face was drawn and thin, masked with a long, dark beard and mustache, streaked with gray. His eyes were barely open, perhaps only vaguely seeing. Though I told him who I was, there was no response, and I doubted that he knew me. Although Alan had tried to warn me about his appearance, the shock and reality of his condition immediately overwhelmed me. An awful tightness suddenly rose in my chest as the tears welled in my eyes. The fact that nothing could be done to save Greg from dying was too much. Logic was gone. Lost in a terrible grief and barely able to see my way to the door of Greg's room, I fled to the Visitor's Lounge.

Later, that day, I started the long drive from Cincinnati back home to Mt. Vernon, Virginia. Two days later, on September 20, 2001 Greg died in hospice care. The following spring, Ginny and I, Frank and his wife Kathy, and Alan and his wife Kittie, gathered at Byron Cemetery in Fairborn, Ohio. Using a lovely pottery urn which Kittie had made and painted, we interred Greg's ashes with those of our parents.

IV

Gregory's birth, life and death represent a profound tragedy. Only recently have I begun to explore and come to some understanding of its emotional and spiritual impact on my life and on the members of my family. The greatest tragedy of all is that our family was insulated from gay people. When it became apparent that Greg was gay, our parents did not know how to react. At one point our father shared with me his wondering as to whether Greg might somehow learn not to be gay. Remember, Greg's teenage and college years were the nineteen fifties. Neither our family, nor the churches my father served, knew how to accept gay people. By the time Dad was able to accept that Greg was gay, the alcoholism had become so pervasive that it became the controlling issue in our parents' struggle to deal with Greg's dependent behavior. Through all of these years, I think Mom suffered in silence, a mother who loved her youngest child dearly, but was powerless to do anything to change the course of his life.

I was angry at my youngest brother's addiction to alcohol and his refusal to seek treatment. The fact that he died an ill and broken person at age fifty-seven was a tragedy which seemed to offer no redeeming grace. What I have learned about the effects of the lack of secure attachment in infancy has helped me see the terrible loss of emotional resources Greg suffered. I have shed agonizing tears over the fact that his early life was so emotionally impaired. In spite of his tragic story, I am able to know two realities that redeem Greg's life. The first is that, I recall him as a youngster who was fun-loving. He had a creative streak, but just at the time that it might have blossomed in college, alcohol began its slow but certain destruction.

The other reality that redeems Greg's life for me is that I have come to new understandings of and support for efforts to increase the acceptance of gay, lesbian, bi-sexual and transgendered people. In October of 1991, about a month after Greg's death, I wrote a letter to our congregation in support of the proposal to become an Open and Affirming congregation in the United Church of Christ, thus affirming and welcoming LGBTQ people. I was preaching at another church on the day of the vote. The congregation's vote to be an Open and Affirming was nearly unanimous in the affirmative.

Subsequently, in July of 2005, I was a delegate to the General Synod, the national biennial meeting of the UCC. I cast my vote in favor of the resolution supporting marriage equality, an action I took in memory and honor of Greg. On this day my tears were a mix of sadness, in remembrance of my brother, and joy about affirming the right to marry who one loves. My vote honored a brother whose life inspired me, in concert with many other friends and mentors, to expand my own understandings and commitments to equal treatment for all people. I try to speak against intolerance in the places where I encounter it in this broken and imperfect world. Gregory helped me be one voice among many voices who have helped to open wider the doors of inclusion and radical hospitality.

FRANK CARIS PETERS
APRIL 6, 1940 – JUNE 24, 2013

Frank's wife, Kathy, asked me to assist the planning of the Service of Thanksgiving and Celebration for my brother's life and to lead it. My tribute was prepared with this dual role in mind. The service was held in the chapel at First Congregational Church in Eugene, Oregon on October 16, 2013.

I

We have gathered to give thanks for and celebrate the life of Frank Caris Peters. His middle name was our mother's family name. Kathy, Alan and I planned this celebration as a time to acknowledge both the pain of our loss and the wonderful gifts that came to us from this fascinating guy who was brother, husband, uncle, cousin and friend.

A few selected lines from Psalm 150 (*New Oxford Annotated Bible*) provide the background for my reflections. The words include a reference that will become more apparent in a few moments. The psalmist wrote:

> 1 Praise the Lord!
> Praise God in the sanctuary;
> Praise him in his mighty firmament!
> 3 Praise God with Trumpet sound,
> praise God with lute and harp!
> 6 Let everything that breathes praise
> The Lord!

It has been a challenge for me to prepare an appropriate remembrance of Frank's life. After several attempts, I realized that a quirk of history has created the problem. Through no fault of my own, I was the first-born and therefore the oldest of four sons of Robert and Mary Peters. By another quirk of circumstance, it was three years before Frank came along to confront me with my first sibling. Now, I can't say that that event was the start of a sibling rivalry, but I can't speak for my brothers' perspectives.

The four of us Peters boys as kids came to be known as the Petey boys, a less harsh-sounding formulation of the family name. Perhaps it was applied to all four of us because "Petey" was Frank's nickname in our early years, one he did not like! And so, we all came to share it. I have to admit that, as the oldest of the four of us, I knew too little of the experiences of the others once I went to college and divinity school.

II

Even so, let me share some recollections you may appreciate. They come from the years in Sandusky, Ohio when our father was the minister at the First Congregational Church. In Junior High, I got interested in the band and began playing the baritone horn. It was almost as big as I was. Every day, in seventh and eighth grade, I could be seen, all ninety pounds of me, lugging my baritone horn in its black case for the six blocks to home. My books were under my other arm since we didn't use backpacks in those days! When Frank got to junior high, he wanted to be in the band too. But he got smart! He chose the trumpet. When I was a senior and he a freshman, we both toted out instruments back and forth every day.

We shared another activity. We both had Sunday morning newspaper routes delivering the *Cleveland Plain Dealer*. We each had a customer list of about thirty-five homes, and a heavy load of Sunday papers to get delivered. They were too bulky to carry in a bag over our shoulders on our bikes. We stacked the papers in the trunk and half of the back seat of the car, crammed one of us in back and one in the passenger seat. Dad would drive us, and we walked the papers to the doors rain or shine. Now mind you, Dad then had to get home, get dressed for church and take us with him to church for Sunday School and the service. But those Sunday paper routes, and my daily afternoon route with the local paper, earned us a lot of money for college.

One other story comes from the summer of 1950 when our parents planned a trip to California to attend a church meeting and visit aunts, uncles and cousins. Dad's interest in the story of the American expansion into The West meant that he planned the trip to include visits to pioneer sites on the Oregon Trail as well as sites which had been important in the story of encounters between Native Americans and the U.S. government. Imagine four young boys, ages 6 to 13, in the back seat of a 1950 Ford sedan for a week-long trip. There were some cantankerous moments in a car without air conditioning. But we survived.

This trip prompted Frank's life-long interest in the history and fate of Native Americans. Subsequently, he wrote his required high school research term paper about the native peoples of the West, focused especially on the Sioux Nation, and it stirred his convictions about oppression and justice in his adult life. It also led to his deep interest in the Lewis and Clark Expedition to explore the Louisiana Purchase.

III

Frank endured a variety of health challenges. He bore the regimen of thrice-weekly dialysis with dignity and a determined matter-of-fact approach. He appeared to maintain good humor throughout it all. Without Kathy's enduring support, he would have been much less comfortable and secure. I'm sure there were days when both he and Kathy wished that the situation was not what it was. But they carried on with a determination to live as fully as possible, each supporting and loving the other.

My brother loved words. For him, words had the power to express the essence of things. He was always wanting the right word. One of the key disciplines in the study of ancient texts, is word study, the effort to discover the precise, original meaning of a word. Frank was always looking for precise meanings! As a scholar, he could read Aramaic, the language of Jesus, Syriac, Biblical Hebrew, Acadian, Ugaritic, and as he said, "a very little Arabic." No wonder he was always looking for the precise meaning of a word!

There is a trait among humans to which Frank was particularly averse. He disliked individuals who enjoyed exhibiting the trait. These are folks he deemed "dunces." But he meant the term in its original meaning, not its modern, altered meaning. I found the original term in a little book I gave Frank. It is titled *Anonyponymous: the Forgotten People Behind Everyday*

Words. An eponym is a word which derives from a particular person's name.

Well, the word "dunce" comes from the Scottish theologian Duns Scotus (yes, Duns is pronounced "dunce"). In 1508, the theological ideas of Duns Scotus about the Immaculate Conception were disputed by the followers of Thomas Aquinas. The Scotists stuck doggedly to their ideas in spite of losing credibility in the face of newer thinking. To be called a "dunce" became an insult hurled at anyone unwilling to learn new ideas. Frank could not abide those he deemed "dunces" – folks who stuck doggedly to an idea regardless of evidence to the contrary. Frank reserved the term primarily for politicians rather than theologians – I wonder why? The modern meaning has strayed far from the original.

IV

Frank's life, his studies in the Hebrew scriptures and his unassuming way were, to me, a life lived with the quiet assurance that there is a loving God, one Frank knew through his intense study of the texts. His praise and faith were not the sounding of a trumpet. Rather, he chose to be content in understanding, as best he could, the prophets and poets of the Hebrew texts. These were the texts which were the wellspring from which came the ministry of Jesus of Nazareth. Frank believed a person could not understand Jesus without understanding the faith tradition into which Jesus had been born and which he tried so fervently to reform. It is a faith tradition that has shaped us all to one degree or another.

I will cherish the brother and scholar who was, and will always be, the second brother of the Petey boys. Each of us here today has been enriched by our experience of knowing and loving Frank. We are blessed by his gifts. May the memory of his vitality be with us always. And remember the source of the word "dunce." Amen.

The poem on the following page was written several days after I returned home from Oregon. It was inspired by the location Frank and Kathy chose for scattering a portion of his ashes.

Commendation at McKenzie Pass*

Five million years ago, before speech,
This globe, wheeling through its galaxy,
Spewed pyroclastic mayhem,
And birthed a rock-strewn, basalt landscape
Devoid of life.
Found by native peoples
An instant ago in volcanic time,
'Tis barren and void still,
Visited in wonder by the curious,
the enthralled, the theological,
Musing in myriad ways over
the cataclysmic enormity
Spreading beyond the reach of human eyes.
And we, grief-stricken and lost,
Bring what's left of your mortality,
Ashy and urn-packed,
To scatter among the rock-hard black basalt
Of God's eternity
While our tears pour out
The unending loss of a husband, brother,
Uncle, cousin and friend
Whose life seems now but a nanosecond of
Creation time.
Scholar of the ancients,
Explorer of the Hebrew texts,
You knew the psalmist said
Our lives are three score and ten,
Or by reason of longevity, four score.
So we grieve,
Bound to you by unbroken love,
Reaching beyond ash urn and volcano
To the everlasting infinity of God,
The Great Spirit.
V'yanauch b'shalom l'netsach,
Rest in peace eternally.

---

*McKenzie Pass is located amid a huge expanse of hardened black lava in the Cascade
Range in Oregon. Frank was a Biblical scholar.

ALAN STUART PETERS
MAY 22, 1944 – JULY 1, 2016

I

A memorial service and celebration of
Alan's life was held at Shepherd of the Hills
Community Church in Murphy, North Carolina
on July 7, 2016.

APPRECIATE THE OPPORTUNITY TO SHARE A BRIEF PERSPECTIVE ABOUT MY BROTHER, A GENUINELY LOVING, CARING, ENTHUSIASTIC MAN WITH A HEARTY AND INFECTIOUS LAUGH. In our youth, Alan and I had a complex relationship. There were moments when we were seriously at odds. Most of it was the product of the normal back-and-forth one would expect in a family of four rambunctious boys. Each of us carried the title of PK – preacher's kid.

As you may imagine, everyone in the Congregational churches our father served expected that, somehow, these four PKs had been blessed with an extra gene that equipped us to be special examples of good behavior, deportment and seriousness. That assumption was somewhat misguided. We could be rambunctious! A story illustrates the point.

When Dad would go out of town to a denominational meeting of some sort, Mom was left to manage us boys. One evening, bedtime became a bit of a hassle. Although we had properly prepared for bed, the call "lights out" did not bring the desired result. A good bit of out-of-bed horseplay was going on. In spite of several warnings, the ruckus continued. Suddenly, the call came from downstairs: "Boys, come down here, now!"

Slowly we trudged down the stairs. An obviously unhappy mother sent us to the dining room. The lights were on. All became clear when she directed us to "march around the table until I tell you to stop." The first steps were somewhat slow. "Faster." she said. Again: "Faster." Now we were speed-walking around the dining room table and beginning to get winded. Mom asked if we had had enough. When we said "yes," she relieved us of the ordeal, and sent us to bed with our promise that we would go to sleep.

Here's the best part: that same table, built by our father over 70 years ago, has been the gathering place in Alan and Kitties' home this week, once again helping us through another significant event in all our lives.

II

A half dozen years after our dining room run, Alan put his running skills to good use when he became the athlete of the family. He played halfback on the Sandusky, Ohio High School football team and later at Shaw High in East Cleveland. When he had the ball, pity the person who got in his way. He simply put his shoulder down and ran over the tacklers.

Before long, I was through college and off to seminary. Our paths diverged as I began a family and career, and experienced several job changes. Along the way, each of us Peters boys faced our own struggles.

I didn't begin to re-connect in a serious way with Alan until the late 1980s. By now, Ginny and I were in Chattanooga and Mom and Dad were living near Crossville, Tennessee. Alan and I were brought together in the fall of 1989 by a mutual desire to support each other as we both walked the road to recovery from addiction. And in the midst of that experience, we faced the reality that our Dad was diagnosed with lung cancer.

When Dad faced several days of radiation treatments at Erlanger medical center, Alan came from Macon to be with him in the hotel adjacent to the hospital. Once again, Alan put his head down, and let nothing stand in the way of caring for Dad. Several years later, he did the same with Mom. After she broke her hip, Alan got her into a rehab center in Macon and looked after her.

Alan's career took many turns. But the final one took him back to teaching. He became a teacher of children with significant special needs. It was work he loved. It required great compassion, as well as patience. To this day, I stand in awe of what he accomplished in those years. To me, nothing expresses Alan's character more clearly than his work equipping those challenged youngsters to be the best they could be, and assuring them that they were loved and valued.

It reminds me of the second aspect of Alan's athletic career. In the spring, he ran track. His event was the low hurdles. I'm amazed that any person can run and jump well enough to go over those obstacles without knocking them all over. Even if a runner did knock one down, he or she kept going. That's how I see Alan's life. *He kept going.*

And then he cleared his greatest hurdle of all, and in the process, he found the love that became his joy-filled, let's-meet-the-challenges-together marriage to Kittie. Their partnership and happiness have also given us great joy, knowing that the two of them found a deep affection that lasted a quarter of a century. And after they moved to Murphy, they found the fellowship of this caring church. Alan found another way to express his deep-seated concern for others. He became a volunteer and for many years was the president and operating manager of the very effective community food pantry, the Caring Center in Murphy. His service was long, helping to feed hundreds of hungry families.

You see, there are things that rub off on you when you are a PK. Alan learned how to be concerned for the well-being of others. I believe all those hours in Sunday School, along with the nurture from our parents and caring church people, established an inner resource that became part of his fundamental character, his core. Along the way, he and I made some wrong choices, and we had to find our way back. By the grace of God, we were receptive to opportunities for change, and willing to listen to the leading of God and caring people. For Alan and Kittie, this meant the opportunity to create a marriage and a home that enriched not only the two of them, but also the community in which they lived and the children and grandchildren they have nurtured.

There is one other thing about Alan I will share, this one with Kittie's permission. I think most of us realize Alan was an unassuming person. He didn't worry about appearances. When he was working around the house and yard, he probably had on a pair of rather threadbare, baggy jeans and an equally tired shirt, and maybe a slouch hat. At home, one wouldn't think much of his "hobo look" as Kittie called it. But if in the midst of such a workday, he needed to go to town or stop at the Caring Center, he went without a thought for what he looked like.

One day, Kittie decided she had had enough and her sense of humor took over. She made a little cardboard medallion. It's like one of those medallions which separate the sizes on a clothes rack. Kittie went to their closet, pushed all of Alan's so-called hobo-looking clothes to one end of the clothes bar and put the medallion in front of them. She added a message. She drew a circle with a slash through it and wrote this instruction: "Work Clothes: Do Not Wear in Public!" Knowing my brother, and the strength of their relationship, I suspect Alan took it all in stride and kept wearing his favorite "hobo clothes" anyway, without concern for what others might think.

Yes, Alan was one of a kind. We acknowledge our grief and loss and commend him to God's eternal care. We do so in the sure and certain knowledge that, from the day he was born, he was in the care of God's unfailing love, as each one of us is. May God bless Alan and each of us, this day and forever. Amen.

CONCLUDING THOUGHTS

My journey in therapy, over a period of almost nine years, began with what I thought was a simple inability to be motivated. Instead, I encountered an incredible story of childhood trauma. In the end, the process enabled me to identify and understand my feelings of anger, grief and disappointment over losses I and my brothers suffered. Given the fact that three of the four of us boys appear to have inherited a genetic tendency toward addiction, it seems that Greg was virtually guaranteed to fall victim to using alcohol in an attempt to ease the pain he must have felt trying to relate to those around him without having the emotional resources to do so. I grieve the fact that he was not able to live openly in a world which is moving beyond the oppression of the 1950s and 1960s, but still has not achieved true equality for all people. I love my youngest brother, forgive his addiction and commend him to the grace of God's unceasing love.

An important outcome of this work has been the realization that the image of our family my father wanted to project became one I am not able to sustain. Throughout his life, I believe he wanted the outside world, and particularly the people in the congregations he served, to believe that ours was a model family, and that we four boys were destined to be leaders in our professions. It did not turn out that way. Each of us faced most of our greatest difficulties after our educations were in their final stages, and after Dad moved to a new phase of his career and was no longer serving in parish ministry.

The impact of our childhood situation led us each to experience the crises which impacted our lives and careers in both positive and negative ways. I have mourned the losses in all our lives. I do give Mom and Dad great credit for insuring that each of us succeeded in earning a college degree. All four of us went on to achieve Master's degrees. Greg earned his Master's degree in Library Science, and Alan achieved his in Education. Frank earned both a Bachelor of Divinity degree and a Master of Sacred Theology degree. Still, each of us struggled in our careers.

Clearly, the trauma of my mother's illness and the threat to her life was an experience which altered my attachment with my Mom. It also created changes in how I approach and deal with others. Throughout my working years, I found it difficult to deal with people in authority. I tended to doubt my ability to perform satisfactorily for employers and wondered if I really measured up in the eyes of others. I tended to doubt I was loveable. This journey has helped me be aware of my inner critic, and I now know the roots of my tendency toward introversion. The nature of my attachment "style" in significant ways.

The deep grief over my mistaken belief about not being wanted has been relived and healed. I simply know and acknowledge it as an element in my life. The little boy who stood in the middle of the church's big, empty room beneath the sanctuary yearning for his mother, not wanting to sit with the Baileys, has been heard and comforted. As an adult, I am able to recognize ways in which my moods and emotions are triggered, and I have developed mindful awareness of the situations which trigger depression. Equally important, I know the steps for mitigating the onset of a down mood. I have found new sources of enjoyment. Writing is one. Occasional teaching is another. I continue to enjoy my woodworking hobby. The study of the Christian mystics is a continuing source of new insights. A new world of spirituality and contemplative prayer is open to me.

In the summer of 2009, in great emotional pain, I asked Dr. A. two questions: *Where did all this sadness come from? Will I ever feel happy again?* Dr. A.'s response was "It is the answers to those questions we will explore together." We have done so, and I am grateful for the journey, and for the help of my PTS therapist. She, too, knew how to reach and heal my pained inner child. I appreciate the sensitive and able work of these two therapists. They helped me confront the most difficult challenges of our work. They have guided me to a new place of peace.

As the surviving member of my family of origin, I have been able to discover and own the core realities of my life and the family into which I was born. For my sons and grandchildren and my only nephew, I hope and trust they will come to understand at least some of the story which is a part of their heritage. The journey continues and the canvas of my life is not yet complete.

L. to R. Frank, Gregory, Alan, and Rob at Frank's wedding, August 19, 1967

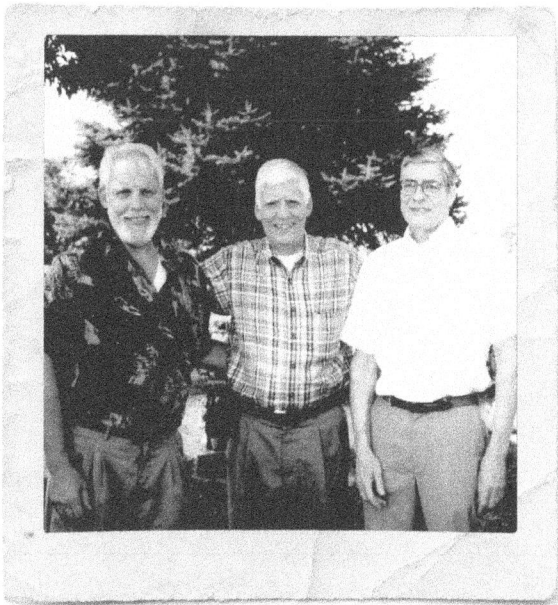

L. to R. Alan, Rob, Frank, after interment
of Greg's Ashes, May 2002

Bibliography

Anonymous, *The Cloud of Unknowing*, *(New York, Harper Collins Press; original copyright by Paulist Press, Mahwah, NJ,)*1981.

Bourgeault, Cynthia, *Centering Prayer and Inner Awakening*, (Lanham, MD, Cowley Publications), 2004.

Bowlby, John, *Attachment*, (New York, Basic Books), 1969.

Goleman, Daniel, *Emotional Intelligence: Why It Can Matter More Than IQ*, *(New York, Bantam Books,)* Tenth Anniversary Addition, 2005.

Lovenheim, Peter, *The Attachment Effect: Exploring the Powerful Ways Our Earliest Bond Shapes Our Relationships and Lives*, (New York, Penguin Random House), 2018.

Nouwen, Henri J. M., *The Return of the Prodigal Son*, (New York, Bantam Doubleday Dell Publishing), 1992.

Nouwen, Henri, J. M., *The Wounded Healer*, (New York, Image Doubleday, second edition,) 1992.

Nouwen, Henri J. M., *Life of the Beloved*, (New York, Crossroad Publishing), 1992.

Williams, Mark, et al., *The Mindful Way Through Depression: Freeing Yourself from Chronic Unhappiness*, (New York, The Guilford Press), 2007.

www.ingramcontent.com/pod-product-compliance
Lightning Source LLC
Chambersburg PA
CBHW022008100426
42736CB00041B/1049